POLL BOOKS
c1696-1872:
A DIRECTORY TO HOLDINGS IN GREAT BRITAIN

Jeremy Gibson and Colin Rogers

THIRD EDITION

Federation of Family History Societies

Published by the
Federation of Family History Societies,
c/o The Benson Room, Birmingham and Midland Institute,
Margaret Street, Birmingham B3 3BS, England.

First edition, 1989.
Second edition, 1990.
Third edition, 1994.

Copyright © Federation of Family History Societies, 1994,
on behalf of the compilers, Jeremy Gibson and Colin Rogers.

ISBN 1 872094 85 6

Cover and title page graphics by Linda Haywood.
Cover illustration: details from Hogarth's 'The Polling'.

Typeset in Arial from computer discs prepared by Jeremy Gibson
and printed by Parchment (Oxford) Limited.

ACKNOWLEDGMENTS

As with other Guides on which we have collaborated, the suggestion to compile *Poll Books* came from Colin Rogers, and the bulk of the work has been done by him: composing the questionnaire sent to hundreds of libraries and record offices, collating the replies, dealing with correspondence and writing most of the introduction.

Jeremy Gibson sent out the questionnaire and researched the collections at the Bodleian Library and the British Library. He has arranged the Guide in its present form and freshly prepared the computer disc from which this third edition has been typeset.

Once again we are indebted to many libraries and archivists throughout the country who have responded to our enquiries. We hope the Guide will confirm them in their appreciation of the rarity of many poll books in their collections, and also stimulate photocopying of them to enhance holdings elsewhere.

We are grateful too to those who helped us by checking individual collections: staff at the Institute of Historical Research, particularly Clyve Jones, and the Guildhall Library; Marilyn Hayward (Cambridge University Library) and Michael Farrar (for securing this help); Sheila Rowlands (National Library of Wales); and Marjorie Kennedy (various Edinburgh repositories). We have also made much use of L.W. Lawson Edwards' catalogue of the collection at the Society of Genealogists.

This third edition incorporates the usual minor alterations, corrections and additions, of which the most significant are the collections at Warwick Library and (brought to our attention by John Hebden) York Minster Library. Mark Pack helpfully told us of various references to poll books in *Papers of British Politicians, 1782-1900* (RCHM, 1989). We are always pleased to hear of additional copies of poll books and new publications and, of course, are grateful to be told of the inevitable occasional error.

Maps of England and Wales showing parliamentary representation before and after 1832 are from G.T. Warner, C.H.K. Martin and D.E. Muir, *The New Groundwork of British History* (1943), reproduced by kind permission of Blackie and Son Ltd. That of Wales alone is from A.J. James and J.E. Thomas, *Wales at Westminster: A History of the Parliamentary Representation of Wales 1800-1979* (1981), reproduced by kind permission of Gomer Press.

J.S.W.G. and C.D.R.

INTRODUCTION

To historians in our own century, brought up to regard the secret ballot as the only legitimate way to test a population's political preferences, poll books offer an extraordinary and anachronistic window onto the electoral practices of our predecessors because they record the names of the candidates for whom they voted. While some exist from before the last decade of the seventeenth century (though they must not be confused with books in which the poll tax was recorded), it was largely the Act of 1696 (7 & 8 W.III c.25) which supposedly gave the main impetus to their publication. This provided that sheriffs were responsible for compiling a record of the poll in *county* elections, and that returning officers should make that record available to anyone wishing to have access to it; a further Act of 1711 (10 Anne c.23) confirmed the onus to maintain a record of the residence and freehold of electors, and enacted that it should be handed over to the Clerk of the Peace for permanent preservation. Only in 1843 were similar measures passed for the preservation of *borough* election records, but in one of those unbelievable acts of archival vandalism with which our records have been afflicted from time to time, the entire collection of the consequent manuscript poll books was destroyed in 1907.

For most, if not all, of the period until the 1872 Ballot Act (35 & 36 V. c.33) which effectively ended them (only the University constituencies being exempted), the clerks themselves were not responsible for publication. Even the earliest printed poll books, which were on the whole for counties rather than boroughs, were brought out by private entrepreneurs who felt themselves to be reasonably sure of a profit. Prospective purchasers were apparently far more numerous than those directly involved in local politics, and there is some evidence, from the nineteenth century at least, that businessmen were prepared to enquire into the political inclinations of prospective trading partners. The rate of publication seems to have varied across the country; there seems to be no obvious explanation as to why there are none for the counties of Cornwall or Somerset, or for the North Riding of Yorkshire.

Content

From the early eighteenth century, it is normal to find only the name and parish of each voter, especially in the original manuscript poll books. However, it is impossible to generalise about what additional information is likely to be published, though there is a suspicion that the content of an earlier poll book from the same constituency was often taken as a model -- where unusual elements are found, they are often repeated in the next poll book(s). Quite commonly published are voters' occupations and qualifications, indicating the basis on which they were entitled to vote, with freemen or £10 householders sometimes identified as such, more rarely with the occupiers of their freeholds. The Chester poll book of 1818 lists voters first under streets and separately under trades. 'Out voters' -- those who did not live in the constituency -- are often listed. Others occasionally distinguished are those who had taken official oaths, members of corporations, burgesses, clergy, and recently admitted ratepayers.

Rarely, Dissenters are identified (as at Abingdon in 1734), or Catholics (Preston, 1807). Paupers, not always remembered as possible voters before the twentieth century, are distinguished in the 1816 Gloucester by-election; those guilty of personation in a series of Bristol elections, 1837-47; and, at Great Yarmouth, those who had promised to vote for one candidate in the election of 1854 and then had not done so! Change of political allegiance was noted at Grimsby in 1818, Canterbury in 1847 and Leicester in 1852.

Electors who had not voted were often singled out for attention. At Boston in 1865, even ill voters are listed, and at Hull in 1847 those who were at sea. It is not clear why some poll books identify those electors who, when the hustings remained open for several days, voted on the last possible day. Perhaps they were considered waiverers, and thus legitimate targets for propaganda at the next election.

Noted below are the activities of political agents in minimising the number of opposition voters on the register. (Their work can be seen in a few surviving canvassers' books, in which the electorate's vote at the last election can usually be found, as well as their declared intentions for the next; see the illustration on page 10.) Many poll books make a note of those who had been omitted from the register as a result of these objections, together with the reasons for their exclusion and sometimes their voting intentions!

For genealogists there is the all too occasional excitement of the names of the fathers of some voters being provided by poll books at Lancaster, Newcastle under Lyme, and Stafford.

Normally, all voters are listed, though if a political party was responsible the accuracy of the publication will always be questionable, and sometimes, voters for only one party or candidate are listed. Try to note if the background documents -- speeches, for example -- are rather one-sided! The names of candidates are shown (rarely their addresses, and more rarely still their political party), the result of the poll, and quite often an account of the proceedings of the event, speeches, and occasionally the voting history of the constituency. Indexes are often provided, unless voters are presented in alphabetical order. Occasionally, a map of the constituency was included, as in Lincolnshire, 1818.

No attempt has been made in this Guide to indicate the heads of information contained in individual poll books. Full details are already provided for all those that have been printed in John Sims' excellent and authoritative *Handlist of British Parliamentary Poll Books* (1984). This reference book is now out of print, but should be consulted by anyone with 'in depth' interest in the subject. Our Guide differs in two important aspects: whereas Sims usually only indicates two repositories, one in London and another locally, we have attempted to show all publicly available holdings; we have also included manuscript poll books, omitted by Sims. Like him we have excluded Ireland, for which (1832-1872) there is already a published list (Walker and Hoppen, 1976).

It should be assumed that, apart from name, residence, qualification, and recorded votes of each elector, data was almost certainly entered by the publisher, not by the returning officer or hustings clerk. Hence, the results of the elections found in poll books need to be treated with caution, and official results be sought in Craig (1973, 1977) and Vincent and Stenton (1971).

Many poll books now found in libraries have been annotated by their original owners, sometimes with previous voting inclinations for each voter, for example, and in one case (one of the British Library copies of Liverpool 1830) the recipients of £22,360 worth of bribes paid during the election!

Janet Seaton's *English Constituency Histories 1265-1832* provides a much more comprehensive range of printed sources than those listed in our first edition. In the second and this edition we have omitted most such references, retaining only those not mentioned by her.

Who voted?

The fine detail of the law relating to the right to vote before the twentieth century is rather complex, and anyone wishing to pursue particular circumstances is directed to works such as Cox and Grady, *Rogers on Elections*, or Seager (1881). A simplified version follows.

Until the end of the period during which poll books were published, the three types of constituency (county, borough and university) had quite different franchise histories, and the Scottish franchise was different again. Note that some towns were technically counties, and therefore came under the county franchise legislation. They were Berwick upon Tweed, Bristol, Exeter, Haverfordwest, Lichfield and Nottingham.

In *counties* the right to vote was given in 1429 to all men of 21 or over having freehold lands or tenements whose annual net value was 40s. or more; until 1774, such voters had to reside in the county in which that land or tenement was situated. From about 1780 to 1832, payment of Land Tax on such property was a convenient qualification; consequently the Clerks of the Peace retained duplicates of the tax assessments which often survive in Quarter Sessions records (see Gibson, Medlycott and Mills, 1993). The pre-1832 franchise in Scotland was narrower than in England and Wales, as the county '40s.' freehold was taken as the value as it had been at the end of thirteenth century, but increased through inflation to some £70.

The 1832 Reform Act (2 & 3 Will.IV c.45) extended the county franchise by giving the vote to:

a) anyone having a life interest in, and occupation of, lands or tenements worth over £2 and under £5 per annum;

b) all other holders of real property worth at least £10, a figure reduced to £5 by the 1867 Reform Act (30 7 31 V. c.102); 1867 also gave the vote to occupiers (owners or tenants) of lands or tenements paying rent of £50 *per annum* or more.

In *boroughs* before 1832, the franchise varied widely according to local custom, an extensive electorate in Preston, for example, contrasting with that in the 'pocket boroughs' such as Old Sarum, Wiltshire, where the M.P. was elected by only eleven voters in 1802-3. Such limited franchise applied too to many more populous-seeming places, the 'rotten boroughs', where it might be confined to members of the Corporation. The eighteen aldermen and burgesses at Banbury returned Lord North unopposed throughout his parliamentary career, whilst ensuring regular charitable contributions for the town (and, no doubt, themselves) from his father the Earl of Guilford, who lived nearby (see Jupp 1973; and for the earlier history of borough franchises, see Oldfield 1792).

The 1832 Act standardised this franchise. The right to vote was given to owners or tenants of buildings worth at least £10 per annum, provided they had occupied

1841.

BOROUGH OF BANBURY, IN THE COUNTY OF OXFORD. } LIST OF PERSONS upon the REGISTER OF ELECTORS for the BOROUGH OF BANBURY, on the 30th Day of June.

| H. Holbech. | V. Vincent. | R. Removed. | A. Absent. |
| T. Tancred. | N. Neutral. | D. Deceased. | |

NAMES.	RESIDENCE.	TRADE, PROFESSION, &c.	VOTED FOR		
			H	T	V
Abbott, Thomas	North-bar-street	Grocer	—		
Abraham, James	Fish-street	Tailor		—	
Adkins, William	Market-place	Publican			R
Adkins, John	South-bar-street	Surveyor			R
Allgood, James	Bridge-street	Ironmonger	—		
Amos, Thomas	Bridge-street-south	Butcher	—		
Anderson, James	Parson's-street	Tailor			N
Aplin, Benjamin	Chalcombe	Solicitor	—		
Aplin, Benjamin William	Bridge-street-south	Solicitor	—		
Aplin, John	South-bar-street	Gentleman			A
Appletree, Frederick	South-bar-street	Butcher			R
Armitt, John, senior	Back-lane	Carpenter			R
Armitt, John, junior	High-street	Butcher			N
Arnitt, Samuel, senior	Water-lane	Gardener	—		
Astell, George	Parson's-street	Victualler	—		
Austin, Barnes	South-bar-street	Common Brewer	—		
Austin, John, senior	Bodicote	Mealman	—		
Austin, John, junior	Bodicote	Mealman			N
Bailey, Richard	Market-place	Tailor	—		
Baker, William	Parson's-street	Tailor	—		
Ball, Joseph	Parson's-street	Boot-maker	—		
Ball, Vincent	Parson's-street	Saddler	—		
Barford, John	Market-place	Ironmonger	—		
Barrett, William	Market-place	Maltster	—		
Barton, John	Parson's-street	Jeweller	—		
Baughen, Richard	North-bar-street	Plush-manufacturer	—		
Baughen, Thomas	North-bar-street	Plush-manufacturer	—		
Baxter, Robert	Parson's-street	Shoemaker	—		
Bayliss, Edward	Crouch	Farmer	—		
Bazeley, John	Market-place	Innkeeper			R
Beale, James	South-bar-street	Baker	—		
Bearsley, John	North-bar-street	Plush-manufacturer			D
Beck, William	London-yard	Watchmaker			D
Beere, Thomas	North-bar-street	Grazier	—		
Beere, George	Parson's-street	Tailor			N

A page from the 1841 Poll Book for the Borough of Banbury.

6

it/them for at least twelve months prior to the registration date (15 July annually) and that the appropriate poor rates and assessed taxes had been paid. Residence within seven miles of the borough was essential. This franchise was extended in 1867 to all owners and tenants of dwelling houses (or part thereof if separately rated) and to lodgers paying at least £10 per annum who had lived there for at least twelve months.

This considerable extension of the borough franchise, it is said, made the publication of poll books an uneconomic proposition by the 1870's; yet, as this Guide shows, they continued to be published in substantial numbers of constituencies (except large towns and cities) until the Ballot Act of 1872 (35 & 36 V. c.33).

In certain ancient chartered boroughs, this nineteenth century legislation left untouched some strange anomalies left over from an earlier age: freemen by birth, apprenticeship or descent; 'scot and lot' voters (those who paid poor rates); and 'potwall[op]ers', who occupied a room with a fireplace at which they cooked their own food.

Among the universities, the Convocation of Oxford and the Senate of Cambridge had had the right to elect their own M.P. since the Middle Ages; the graduates forming the convocation of the University of London received the same privilege in 1867.

In all constituencies, there were limitations and disqualifications. Females could not vote in parliamentary elections until the twentieth century. There were legal incapacities which excluded other individuals from the franchise: idiots, lunatics, felons, perjurors, police, postmen, many customs and excise officers, and peers of the realm. Those in receipt of public alms could not vote; nor could aliens, though naturalisation could remove this disqualification after 1870. Anyone convicted of bribery at an election was also disqualified. In 1832, electoral registers (lists of those qualified to vote) were introduced, and since that date, only those who are entered on the annual register have been allowed to vote. (From 1832, the electoral register was often taken as the basis for the poll book itself, which then could show, as at Banbury in 1841, those who were absent, removed, dead, or otherwise politically neutral at the time of the election.) It was therefore in the interest of political agents to ensure that the maximum number of supporters and a minimum number of opponents had their names on the register, a situation which led to considerable ingenuity and skulduggery (see Seymour, 1915/70). Those extant are listed in the companion 'Gibson Guide' to *Electoral Registers since 1832* (Gibson and Rogers, 1990).

Representation

In England, counties were represented by two Members of Parliament, 'Knights of the Shire', until 1832, when many counties were subdivided geographically. Only Yorkshire (whose representation was increased to four in 1821) sent more than two M.P.'s. In Wales, each county had one Knight of the Shire. All but a handful of borough constituencies in England and Wales had two M.P.'s but, through historical accident and the relatively recent growth of some industrial towns, no attempt had been made to relate membership to population, with the result that some very large towns, such as Manchester and Birmingham, were not directly represented. This was partially rectified by the 1832 Reform Act.

PARLIAMENTARY REPRESENTATION BEFORE 1832

BOROUGHS

Boroughs returning two members ●
Boroughs returning one member ○
Boroughs in Wales which shared a member +

Note. (i) London returned four members.
(ii) Melcombe Regis and Weymouth returned four members between them.
(iii) Oxford and Cambridge Universities each returned two members.

COUNTIES

Yorkshire returned four members. All other English Counties returned two members each.
Each Welsh County returned one member.

PARLIAMENTARY REPRESENTATION AS CHANGED BY THE REFORM ACT OF 1832

Boroughs returning two members after 1832 ●   *Boroughs returning one member after* 1832 ○

County members are indicated by numbers. English Counties without numbers returned •
4 members each

Maps opposite and above reproduced from G.T. Warner, C.H.K. Martin and D.E. Muir, *The New Groundwork of British History*, Blackie, 1943. Note that some places are mis-spelt or mis-positioned, and some small boroughs have been overlooked.

No.	Number on Register.	NAME OF ELECTOR.	For whom promised. Milbank / Thompson / Canvas	How voted at last Election Milbank / Thompson / Absent	REMARKS.
	419	Jackson Thomas		✓	
	420	Guig Elisha		✓	on again not for Copy
	421	Lister William		✓	
	422	Lister Wm Junr		✓	
	423	Hartridge Samuel		✓	canvased in hope can Whitby
	424	Marsay Jonathan		✓	neutral - see again
	425	Maw Newton		✓	Outlying Voter
	426	Mead John		✓	
	427	Middleton Wm 688		✓	Outlying V...

A page from a privately owned canvasser's poll book for Graisdale near Whitby, 1868, showing his comments. This appears to be the sole surviving poll book of any sort for the North Riding of Yorkshire, 1832-72.

County and burgh representation in Scotland (from the Act of Union in 1707) was even more complicated. Counties returned one member, but three of the county M.P.'s represented six counties, in rotation. Of the fifteen burgh members, one represented Edinburgh, and the remainder were elected by groups or districts (see Jupp, 1973).

Historical applications

For genealogists and biographers, poll books offer an identification of the way in which specific individuals indicated a voting preference, possibly with additional information about occupations and addresses. The latter, of course, can be very helpful in locating the individuals in census enumerators' returns. In the eighteenth century, pollbooks can be used conveniently for identifying parishes in which people of certain surnames lived.

For family and social historians, voting allegiances across different geographical areas, occupational groups, and even social strata can be studied, all of them over a timescale provided poll books have survived in sufficient numbers. Vincent (1967), for example, gives occupational analyses from some 180 election results. The ownership and tenancy of individual properties can be identified, especially when the data can be used in conjunction with land tax returns or electoral registers.

The political historian has probably exploited these documents more than anyone else, though not as much as one would expect (see Drake, 1974). Particularly since 1970, when the development of computing techniques has allowed for the linkage of thousands of individual voters across different elections and changes of address, the evidence from poll books has allowed an intimate investigation of the mechanisms by which political change has resulted from the swings of opinion by individuals and groups, matching in a way hitherto unachievable in historical periods the politician's modern dependence on (not to say mesmerism with) opinion and exit polls (see Speck et al.).

Record societies have generally ignored the potential for republication of poll books, presuming that because printed copies might exist, they were outside their ambit. This Guide will reveal their rarity, though we hope it may encourage acquisition of photocopies by appropriate libraries and record offices. Just how valuable a modern edition can be made has been demonstrated by the Thoroton Society, whose Nottingham and Nottinghamshire Poll Books for 1710, with biographical index, is a model worthy of emulation.

General Elections 1715 to 1874

1715	1761	1801	1826	1847
1722	1768	1802	1830	1852
1727	1774	1806	1831	1857
1734	1780	1807	1833	1859
1741	1784	1812	1835	1865
1747	1790	1818	1837	1868
1754	1796	1820	1841	1874

Further reading and references

For accounts of specific constituencies, or elections therein, see Janet Seaton's *English Constituency Histories 1265-1832*. A few additional sources not listed by her are located at the relevant point in the text. Unless shown as reprints of poll books, these are unlikely to contain many or any names of voters. No attempt has been made to list the many publications, broadsheets *etc.* about individual elections printed at the time of those elections.

J. Cannon, 'Poll books', *History* **47** (1962).
E.W. Cox and S.G. Grady, *The New Law and Practice of Registration* (various eds., 19th century).
F.W.S. Craig, *The Parliaments of England from 1715 to 1847* (2nd ed., 1973).
F.W.S. Craig, *British Parliamentary Election Results 1832-1885* (1977).
M. Drake, 'The mid-Victorian voter", *Jnl. Interdisciplinary History* **1** (1970).
M. Drake - see Open University.
L.W.L. Edwards (ed.), *Catalogue of Directories and Poll Books in the possession of the Society of Genealogists* (1989).
J.S.W. Gibson, *Local Newspapers 1750-1920: England and Wales; Channel Islands; Isle of Man: a select location list* (1987, updated 1991).
J.S.W. Gibson, Mervyn Medlycott and D. Mills, *Land and Window Tax Assessments* (1993).
J.S.W. Gibson and C.D. Rogers, *Electoral Registers since 1832, and Burgess Rolls: A Directory to holdings in Great Britain* (2nd ed., 1990; 3rd edition in preparation).
E.C. Griffiths, 'A Poll Book analysis package for eighteenth century elections' in P. Denley and D. Hopkin (eds.), *History and Computing* (1987).
D. Hirst, *The Representative of the People? Voters and voting in England under the Early Stuarts* (1975). Provides a list of contested elections, 1604-1640, with sources.
History of Parliament Trust, *Draft Register of Poll Books* (1953).
P. Jupp, *British and Irish Elections 1784-1831* (1973).
D.C. Moore, *The Politics of Deference* (1976).
R.J. Morris, 'Property titles and the use of British urban poll books for social analysis', *Urban History Yearbook* (1983).
T.H.B. Oldfield, *An Entire and Complete History of the Boroughs of Great Britain* (1792).
The Open University, *Introduction to Historical Psephology* (Historical data and the social sciences: D.301, Block 3, Units 9-12) (1974).
Parliamentary History (Year Books, vols. 1-5, 1981-86, Alan Sutton; from 1987 twice yearly, O.U.P).
F.N. Rogers, *Rogers on Elections* (various eds., 19th century).
J.R. Seager, *A Handbook of the Law of Parliamentary Registration* (1881).
Janet Seaton, *English Constituency Histories 1265-1832: A guide to printed sources*, House of Commons Library Document No. **15**, H.M.S.O., 1986.
C. Seymour, *Electoral Reform in England and Wales* (1915, repr. 1970).
J. Sims (ed.), *A Handlist of British Parliamentary Poll Books* (1984).
W.A. Speck and W.A. Gray, 'Computer analysis of poll books: an initial report', *Bulletin of the Institute of Historical Research* **43** (1970).
W.A. Speck, W.A. Gray and R. Hopkinson, 'Computer analysis of poll books: a further report', *B.I.H.R.* **48** (1975).
J.A. Thomas, 'The system of registration and the development of party organisation', *History* **25** (1940).
J.R. Vincent, *Pollbooks: How Victorians Voted* (1967).
J. Vincent and M. Stenton (eds.), *McCalmont's Parliamentary Poll Book 1832-1885* (8th ed., 1971).
B.M. Walker and K.T. Hoppen, 'Irish election poll books, 1832-1872', *Irish Booklore* **3**, 4 (1976, 1980).
B. Williams, 'Was your ancestor a potwalloper?', *Family Tree Magazine* **4**.6 (April 1988).

A note on presentation

For the entire period covered by poll books, Members of Parliament represented whole counties (or, after 1832, part counties), or individual boroughs (apart from the Universities of Oxford and Cambridge and, from 1867 only, London). In this Guide:

Constituencies are in **bold italics**. So far as possible poll books for individual places or areas comprising only part of a constituency are shown as such under that constituency.

Years are those for which printed poll books are known to exist for those constituencies.

Years which are in **bold italics** indicate the survival of a manuscript poll book, the archival repository and reference number (if supplied) normally being provided in such cases.

If there were two elections in the same year, they are distinguished either by an asterisk (indicating a by-election) or by the months of elections being shown.

'Present location unavailable'. The existence of a poll book is known from other sources (private ownership, antiquarian book catalogues *etc.*) but no library or record office has indicated it has a copy.

Years shown in parentheses, *i.e.* (**1715**), indicate an election (or series of elections) about which an article or book has been written, the reference being provided, but do *not* indicate the existence of poll books. Many more such references will be found in *English Constituency Histories 1265-1832*.

Unless otherwise stated, all poll books are for Parliamentary elections.

Abbreviations

The following abbreviations have been used, applicable to all counties.

* = by-election.
AO = Archive(s) Office.
BL = British Library.
BLN = British Library (Newspapers). Consult Sims' *Handlist* (1984) for details; Gibson's Local *Newspapers* (1991) can then be used to discover local holdings of the newspapers concerned.
Bod = Bodleian Library, Oxford. A copy of the History of Parliament's *Draft Register*, annotated with shelf marks for Bodleian holdings, is available in Duke Humfrey's Library (Dept. of Manuscripts).
CL = Central Library (poll books will normally be in Local Studies Departments).
CoL = County Library.
CUL = Cambridge University Library.
GL = Guildhall Library, London. Note that the Library's collection of Poll Books, described in *Handlist of Poll Books in the Guildhall Library*, published in 1926, was destroyed by enemy action during the last war, and that the present collection has been built up since. Public access to poll books may be subject to proof of identity.
IHR = Institute of Historical Research, University of London. The collection includes most printed poll books, or photocopies of books not available elsewhere in London. Original printed copies and photocopies at the IHR are not differentiated in this Guide. Access to the IHR is limited, and the Institute should be approached first to see whether permission to use the collection can be granted.
MF = Microfilm/microfiche.
RO = Record Office.
SoG = Society of Genealogists, 14 Charterhouse Buildings, Goswell Road, London EC1M 7BA (tel. 01-251 8799). Open to non-members, Tues. - Sat. (daily charge).
UL = University Library. Right of access should not be assumed; please contact the Chief Librarian concerned.
var(s) = variant(s), or alternative publication(s) of the same poll. These can vary from bibliographical technicalities to matters of considerable substance; see Sims' *Handlist* (1984) for details.

BEDFORDSHIRE

Abbreviations (national collections, page 14)
BCL = Bedford Central Library.
BRO = Bedfordshire Record Office (MS and publ. not always differentiated).
BTH = Bedford Town Hall (by appointment only; items can be consulted by arrrangement in BRO).

Constituency histories: Seaton (1986), page 12.

County
1685. BRO [CH 922].
1705. BRO, BTH, GL, IHR.
1715. BRO, BTH, Bod, IHR.
1722. BRO, BL, IHR.
1727. BTH, BRO.
1734. BRO.
1774. BCL, BRO, BTH, BL, Bod, IHR; SoG (MS 'Analysis', presumably of printed poll book).
1784. BCL, BRO, BTH, BL, IHR.
1807. BCL, BRO, BTH, BL, GL, Bod, IHR, SoG.
1820. BCL, BRO, BTH, GL, IHR, SoG.
1826. BCL, BRO, BTH, IHR.
1831. BRO, BTH, GL.
1857. BCL, BRO, BTH, IHR.
1859. BCL, BRO, BTH, GL, SoG.
1872*. BRO, BTH, IHR.

Bedford
1640. BRO [T.W.890].
1705. BRO [GY 8/3].
1721. BRO [OR 1818].
1725. BRO [OR 1819].
1727. BRO [OR 1784, 1786].
1730/1. BRO [OR 1817].
1790. BCL, BRO, BTH, Bod, GL, IHR.
1830. BRO, BTH, Bod, IHR.
1832. BTH [G3/4-5], MS poll added to electoral register.
1835. BRO, BTH, IHR.
1837. BCL, BRO, BTH, BL, IHR.
1841, 1847. BCL, BRO, BTH, IHR.
1852. BTH, IHR.
1854*. BLN, IHR.
1857. BCL, BRO, BTH, IHR.
1859. BTH. IHR.
1859*. BRO, BTH, IHR.
1865. BTH, IHR.
1868. BRO (East and West Wards only), BTH, IHR.

BERKSHIRE

Abbreviations (national collections, page 14)
BRO = Berkshire Record Office.
RCL = Reading Central Library (some quoted in Sims not found).
WG = Windsor Guildhall.

Constituency histories: Seaton (1986), page 12.

County
1722. GL.
1727. Bod, Oxon Archives, IHR, SoG.
1768. BRO, RCL, Bod, GL, IHR, SoG.
1796. BRO, RCL, GL, Bod, IHR.
1812. BRO, RCL, Bod, IHR.
1818. BRO, Bod, IHR.
1820. BRO.
1832. GL.
c.1840. East Ilsley district only: BRO [DP.92/28/3].

Abingdon
1734. var. BRO, Bod, IHR.
1754. Oxon Archives, IHR.
1766-1835. Borough elections. BRO.
1768. BRO, Bod, GL.
1830. BRO, Bod, IHR.
1832, 1834. BRO.
1854*. BRO, BL, IHR.
1868. BRO, IHR.

New Windsor
1711. BRO.
1757*. BRO, IHR.
1780. BRO, WG, IHR.
1794*. BRO, BL, GL, IHR.
1802. Windsor Library, BRO, BL, RCL, Bod, GL, IHR, SoG.
1804*. BRO, WG, GL, IHR, SoG.
1806. WG, IHR, SoG.
1832, 1835, 1857, 1863*. BRO, IHR.
1865. IHR.
1868. WG, IHR.

Reading
1678, 1680. RCL (two MSS), BRO.
1689. RCL (four MSS), BRO.
1740*. RCL, IHR.
1754. var. Bod, RCL, IHR.
1768, 1774, 1780, 1782*. RCL, IHR.
1790. BRO, IHR.
1802. RCL, IHR.
1812. RCL.
1812. RCL, IHR.
1820. var. BRO, RCL, GL.
1820. RCL (poll clerk's book).
1826. var's. RCL, Bod, BL, GL, IHR, SoG.
1835. BRO, RCL, GL.
1835. RCL (poll clerk's book).
1837. var. BRO, RCL, Bod, GL.

Berkshire: *Reading* continued
1837. RCL (poll clerk's book).
1841. RCL, IHR (GL copy missing).
1847. RCL, IHR.
1849*. BLN, IHR.
1852. RCL (with MS additions), GL, IHR.
1859. BLN, IHR.
1860*. BLN, IHR.
1865. RCL, IHR.

Wallingford
1820. BRO, IHR.
1832. BRO, IHR, SoG.
1847. RCL, IHR.

BUCKINGHAMSHIRE

Abbreviations (national collections, page 14)
BAS = Buckinghamshire Archaeological Society.
BRO = Buckinghamshire Record Office.
HWCL = High Wycombe Central Library.

Constituency histories: Seaton (1986), page 12.

County
1685. BRO [D/C/3/61, part only].
1700, 1701, 1702. BRO [D/X993].
1705. Bod, GL, SoG.
1710. BRO [D/MH/40/1].
1710. BAS, BRO, Bod, IHR.
1713. BRO (but copy too fragile for use), Bod, GL, IHR.
1722. BRO [PB/1/1-7].
1722. BRO, BL, Bod, CUL, GL, IHR, SoG.
1734. BRO [PB/2/1-6, D/MH/40/2].
1784. BRO [PB/3/1-9,11-12], with typescript index.
1784. var. BAS, BRO, Bod, GL, IHR, SoG (annotated). Available as Microfiche 3 from SoG.
1831. BRO [PB/14/1-11].
1831. BAS, BRO, Bod, GL, IHR, SoG, Manchester UL.
1832. GL.
1839. SoG (index only).
1841. BAS, BRO, IHR.

Aylesbury
1780. BRO [PB/2A/1].
1802. BRO (publ. 1859).
1804*. var. BRO, BL, Bod, GL, BAS, IHR, SoG, Manchester UL.
1807. BRO [PB/5/1-6].
1818. GL.
1818. BAS, BRO, IHR.
1831. BAS, BRO, GL, IHR.
1832. BRO, IHR.
1835. BAS, BRO, IHR.
1839*. BRO (with typescript index), IHR.
1847, 1848*, 1850*. BRO, IHR.
1851*. BRO, IHR, Bradford (Yorks.) District Archives.
1852. var. BAS, BRO, IHR.

Buckinghamshire: *Aylesbury* continued
1857. BRO, IHR.
1859, 1868. BAS, BRO, IHR.

Buckingham
1791-1835. Elections of bailiff and principal burgesses: BRO [29/74/39/1-3].
1832. BRO [AR 29/74 89].
1832. BRO, BL, IHR.
1837. BRO [AR 29/74 89].

Great Marlow
1784. BAS, IHR.
1847. BRO, IHR.

High Wycombe
1832, 1868. HWCL, IHR.

Wendover
1734. BRO [D/MH/40/5,6].
1741. BRO [D/MH/40/18-20], GL (copy).

CAMBRIDGESHIRE

Abbreviations (national collections, page 14)
CCL = Cambridge Central Library.
CRO = Cambridgeshire Record Office, Cambridge.
CUL = Cambridge University Library.
HRO = Huntingdon Branch, Cambridgeshire Record Office.
MUL = Manchester University Library.
NCL = Norwich Central Library.
PDL = Peterborough Divisional Library.

Constituency histories: Seaton (1986), page 12.
A.J. Pye, 'List of Poll books for parliamentary elections', *Jnl. Cambridgeshire FHS*, **1**.5 (Feb. 1978), for Cambridge and Cambridgeshire and **1**.7 (Aug. 1978) for the University of Cambridge.

County
1705. CRO, CUL, GL.
1722. CUL.
1722. CCL, CRO, CUL (with MS additions for 1724), Bod, IHR, SoG. Available as Microfiche 4 from SoG.
1724*. CCL, CRO, IHR.
1780. CCL, CRO, CUL, HRO, BL, Bod, GL, IHR; SoG (also index to non-resident voters).
1802*. var. CCL, CRO, CUL, IHR.
1802. CCL, CUL, Bod, IHR, SoG.
1826. CCL, CRO, CUL, BL, GL, IHR, SoG.
1830. CCL, CRO, CUL, HRO, BL, Bod, GL, IHR, SoG.
1831*. var. CCL, CRO, CUL, BL, Bod, GL, IHR.
1832. CCL, CRO, CUL, Bod, GL, IHR, SoG.
1835. var. CCL, CRO, CUL, GL, IHR, SoG.
1857. var. CCL, CRO, CUL, PDL, BL, IHR, GL, SoG.
1868. CCL, CRO, CUL, HRO, PDL, BL, GL, IHR, SoG.

Cambridgeshire continued
Cambridge
1774. CCL, CRO, IHR.
1776*. CCL, CRO, GL.
1780. CCL, CRO, BL, GL.
1818. CRO.
1818. CCL, CRO, CUL, IHR.
1819*. CUL, IHR.
1819, 1820, 1828*, 1829* * CRO (with additions) [City/PB.49].
1830. Present location unavailable.
1832. var. CCL, CRO, CUL, St John's College Cambridge, BL, IHR. See J.C. Mitchell and J. Cordforth, 'The political demography of Cambridge 1832-1868', *Albion* **4** (1977).
1834*. CCL, CRO, CUL, BL, IHR.
1835. var. CCL, CRO, CUL, GL.
1837. var. CCL, CRO, CUL, BL, Bod, IHR.
1839*. CCL, CRO, CUL, IHR.
1840*. var. CCL, CRO, CUL, BL, Bod, GL.
1841. var. CCL, CRO, CUL, BL, IHR.
1843*. CCL, CRO, CUL, BL, Bod, IHR.
1845*. CCL, CRO, CUL, BL, Bod, GL.
1847, 1852. CCL, CRO, CUL, BL, IHR.
1854*. var. CCL, CRO, CUL, BL.
1857. CCL, CRO, CUL, BL, GL.
1857-60. Election of Corporation (West Barnwell Ward only): CCL.
1859. CCL, CRO, CUL, GL.
1860. Election of Corporation (East Barnwell Ward only): CCL.
1863*. CCL, CRO, CUL, BL, Bod, GL, IHR.
1865. CCL, CRO, CUL, BL, Bod, GL.
1866*. CCL, CRO, CUL, Bod, GL.
1868. var. CCL, CRO, CUL, BL, Bod, GL, IHR.

Cambridge Poor Law Union
1861-1878. Election of Guardians. CRO.

Cambridge University
1727. CRO, CUL, NCL, BL, Bod, GL, IHR.
1780. CCL, CRO, CUL, HRO, Bod, GL, NCL, MUL, IHR.
1784. CCL, CRO, CUL, HRO, BL, Bod, GL, IHR, NCL, MUL, SoG.
1790. CCL, CRO, CUL, Bod, GL, IHR, NCL, SoG.
1806*. CCL, CRO, CUL, BL, Bod, GL, NCL, IHR.
1807. CCL, CRO, CUL, NCL, BL, Bod, GL, IHR, MUL, SoG.
1811* (M.P. and Chancellor) CRO, CUL, NCL, BL, Bod, GL, MUL, SoG.
1816. Election of Registry: CRO, SoG.
1818. Election of Woodwardian Professor: BL, GL.
1822*. CCL, CRO, CUL, NCL, BL, Bod, GL, IHR, MUL, SoG.
1822. Election of Librarian: GL.
1826. CCL, CRO, CUL, NCL, BL, Bod, GL, IHR, SoG.
1827*, 1829*. CCL, CRO, CUL, NCL, BL, Bod, GL, IHR, SoG.

Cambridge University continued
1831. CCL, CRO, CUL, NCL, BL, Bod, GL, IHR, MUL, SoG.
1832. Election of Registrar: BL.
1836. Election of Public Orator: CCL, CRO, BL.
1840. Election of High Steward: CCL, CRO, BL, GL, SoG.
1845. Election of Librarian: GL.
1847. var. CRO, CUL, NCL, BL, Bod, GL, IHR, SoG.
1847. Election of Chancellor: CCL, CRO, BL, GL.
1848. var. Election of Public Orator: CCL, GL.
1854. Election of Esquire Bedell: GL.
1856*. CCL, CRO, CUL, NCL, Bod, GL, IHR, SoG.
1862. Election of Registrar: GL.
1865. Election of Clerk of Rectory of Ovington: GL.
1866. Election of Professor of Zoology: GL.
1868*. CRO, CUL, NCL, BL, GL, IHR.
1869. Election of Public Orator: GL.
1873. Election of Esquire Bedell: GL.
1875. Election of Clerk to Vicarage of Sheepshed: GL.
1876. Election of Public Orator: CCL, CRO.
1882*. CCL, CRO, CUL, NCL, BL, GL, IHR.
1883. Election of Clerk to Rectory of Ovington (2 elections): GL.
1889. Election of Representative to General Council of Medical Education: GL.
1893. Election of Esquire Bedell: GL.

CHESHIRE
Abbreviations (national collections, page 14)
BCL = Birkenhead Central Library.
CCL = Chester Central Library.
CCRO = Chester City Record Office.
CRO = Cheshire Record Office (Mf = available on microfilm).
MUL = Manchester University Library.
SLC = Salisbury Library, University College, Cardiff.
UCNW = University College of North Wales, Bangor (Dept. of MSS.)

Constituency histories: Seaton (1986), page 12.

County
1702. UCNW [Mostyn 8423-6].
1705. IHR; UCNW [Mostyn 8427].
1714. CRO [QDV/1/1-7, Mf].
1722. CRO [QDV/1/8-15, Mf].
1727. BCL, CCRO [Chester Arch. Coll.], GL.
1837, 1841. CRO.

North Cheshire
1832. CRO [QDV/1.32-47, Mf].
1841. CRO [QDV/1/68-83, Mf].

South Cheshire
1832. CRO [QDV/1/16-31, Mf].
1832. BCL, Bod, IHR, SLC.
1836*. BL.
1837. CRO [QDV/1/48-67, Mf].

Cheshire: *South Cheshire* continued
1837. BCL, BL, Bod, IHR.
1841. CRO [QDV/1/84-104, Mf].
1841. BCL, Bod, IHR.

Chester
1732. Elections of Mayor and M.P.: GL.
1733. CCRO.
1733*. GL.
1747. var. CCL, BL, Bod, GL, IHR, SoG.
1767-1826. Duke of Westminster, c/o CRO.
1771. Election of Sheriff: GL.
1784. var. CCL, CCRO, BL, Bod, GL, IHR, MUL, SLC, SoG.
1812. var. BCL, CCL, CCRO, BL, GL, IHR, MUL, SoG, SLC (two editions, one with MS additions).
1818. BCL, CCL, CCRO, BL, GL, MUL, SLC, IHR.
1818. var. Election of Sheriff: BL, GL, MUL, SLC.
1819. Election of Mayor and Sheriff: BL, GL.
1820. CCL, BL, IHR.
1824. SoG.
1824. Election of Sheriff: BL, GL.
1826. var. BCL, CCL, CCRO, BL, Bod, GL, IHR, MUL, SLC, SoG.
1837. CCRO.
1837. BCL, IHR.
1850*, 1857. CCL, IHR.
1859. CCL, GL.
1865. CCL, IHR.

Macclesfield
1830. Election of Town Clerk and Coroner: BL.
1835. BL.

Stockport
1835. Stockport CL [B/KK/2/3/19], IHR.
1847. Stockport CL [B/KK/2/3/19], IHR.

CORNWALL

Abbreviation (national collections, page 14)
CoRO = Cornwall Record Office.

Constituency histories: Seaton (1986), page 12.

County
1710. CoRO [CF 4787].
1772. var. West Devon Area RO, Plymouth [139/4/2 and 297].
1774. CoRO [X 622].
1790. CoRO [PD 208].

Lostwithiel
1790. CoRO [WH 6600].

Mitchel
1672-1714. 'Poll sheets': CoRO [WH 5192].

Truro
1832. BL, GL.

CUMBERLAND

Abbreviations (national collections, page 14)
CaL = Carlisle Library.
CaRO = Cumbria Record Office, Carlisle (published and unpublished holdings undifferentiated).
DHL = Daniel Hay Library, Whitehaven.

County
Constituency histories: Seaton (1986), page 12.
R. Hopkinson, 'The Electorate of Cumberland and Westmorland in the late seventeenth and early eighteenth centuries', *Northern History* **15** (1979).

1722. CaRO.
1768. CaRO (Allerdale Above and Below; Cumberland, Eskdale and Leath Wards, Whitehaven). See R.B. Levis, 'Sir James Lowther and the political tactics of the Cumberland election of 1768', *Northern History* **19** (1983).
1774. CaRO (Allerdale Above and Below, Cumberland and Leath Wards).
1831. CaRO (Egremont only); CaL, GL, IHR.
1832. CaRO.

East Cumberland
1837. CaRO (Alston, Kirkoswald, Longtown, Penrith only).
1841. CaL, IHR.
1868. CaL, GL, IHR, SoG.

West Cumberland
1835. CaRO (Aspatria, Bootle, Keswick only).
1857. CaL, GL, IHR. See 'Poll Book for Western Cumberland, 1857', *Liverpool FHS Journal* **2**.1 (Spring 1978).

Carlisle
1741. CaL.
1774. IHR (CaL in Sims not found).
1786, April*, Dec.* CaL, Bod, IHR.
1816*. var. CaL, CaRO, IHR (MUL, see **1820***).
1818. CaRO.
1820*. CaL, IHR, MUL (also contains the **1816** poll).
1826, 1827, 1829. CaRO.
1832. CaL.
1837. CaRO.
1847. var. CaL, CaRO, Bod, GL, IHR.
1848*, 1852. CaL, IHR.
1857, 1859. CaL, CaRO, IHR.
1861. var. CaL, CaRO, IHR.
1865, 1868. CaL, IHR.

Cockermouth
1660, 1700, 1701, 1702, 1705, 1710, 1711, 1713, 1717, 1727, 1737, 1738, 1832, 1833, 1835, 1841. CaRO.
1852. var. CaL, IHR.
1868. CaL, IHR.

Whitehaven
1768. CaRO.
1832. CaL, DHL, Bod, IHR.
1868. CaL, DHL, IHR.

DERBYSHIRE

Abbreviations (national collections, page 14)
ChL = Chesterfield Library.
DCL = Derby Central Library.
DRO = Derbyshire Record Office, Matlock.
IL = Ilkeston Library.
MLS = Matlock Local Studies Library.
NUML = Manuscripts Dept., University of Nottingham.
NUL = Nottingham University Library.
SRO = Sheffield Record Office.

Constituency histories: Seaton (1986), page 12.

County
***1656, 1658, 1661** and **n.d. (1670)**.*
DRO [D 258/60/5,28].
1689. DRO [D 258/48/27].
1701. DRO [D 258/48/27], SRO [OD 1181].
1701. DRO (Crown Bar only) [D 208 Z/Z1].
1720/1. SRO [OD 1182].
1734. DRO [D 434 Z/Box 32].
1734. var. Bod, GL, MLS, NUL, IHR, SoG.
1767. NUML (votes promised in Denby, Belper, Morley, and Heage) [DR E 33/17]; (list of voters in Liberty of Spondon) [DR E 33/19-20].

(1832-1865). See C.E. Hogarth, 'The Derbyshire parliamentary elections of 1832', *Derbyshire Arch. Jnl.* **89** (1969); 'The 1835 elections in Derbyshire', *D.A.J.* **94** (1974); 'Derby and Derbyshire elections 1837-47', *D.A.J.* **95** (1975); and 'Derby and Derbyshire elections 1852-65', *D.A.J.* **101** (1981).

East Derbyshire
1868. DCL, GL, IHR.

North Derbyshire
1832. DCL, GL, SoG.
1837. ChL, DCL, IHR, SoG (part).
1853*. DCL, IHR, SoG.
1868. DRO [D 059 Z/Z1].
1868. ChL, DCL, GL, MLS, IHR.
1868. NUML (Baslow and Chatsworth area (?)) [Wr D 13/24].
n.d. (19th cent.) DRO (Hope only) [D 1038 A/PC17].

South Derbyshire
1832. var. IHR.
1835. DCL, Bod, GL.
1841. DCL, IL, IHR, SoG (with MS additions).
1857. DCL, GL, SoG.
1859. DCL, IL, GL, IHR.
1865. DCL, Bod, GL, IHR, SoG, NUL.
1868. DCL, MLS, GL, IHR, SoG, NUL.
1869*. DCL, MLS, GL, IHR, SoG, NUL (copy has **1868** also).

Derby
1698. SRO [EM 1286].
1701. DCL.
1710, 1727. DCL, IHR.
1734. DRO [D 215 Z/Z1].
1734*. DCL.

Derby continued
1734. DCL, IHR.
1741/2*. var. DCL, Bod, GL, IHR.
1748. SRO [OD 1379].
1748*. DCL, IHR.
1772. DCL (also a canvass book and a separate list of out-voters).
1774. DCL (also a canvass book).
1775. DCL.
1775*. var. DCL, Bod, IHR.
1832. IHR.
1835. DCL, IHR.
1837. Voting intentions: DCL.
1837. GL.
1841. DCL, GL.
1847. DCL, IHR, NUL, SoG.
1848*. GL. IHR.
1852. DCL, IHR.
1859. DCL, GL.
1865. Bod, IHR.

DEVON

Abbreviations (national collections, page 14)
DRO = Devon Record Office, Exeter.
ECL = Exeter Central Library.
NDA = North Devon Athenaeum, Barnstaple.
NDRO = North Devon Area Record Office, Barnstaple.
WDRO = West Devon Area Record Office, Plymouth.

Constituency histories: Seaton (1986), page 12.

County
1712. DRO [51/1/1-5]; published in *Trans. Devonshire Association* **106** (1974).
1790. WDRO [74/824].
1816. DRO [51/2/1-10].
1818. DRO [51/3/1-15].
1820. DRO [51/4/1-15].
1826. DRO [51/5/1].
1830. DRO [51/6/1-15].

Barnstaple
1802-41 (with gaps). NDRO [Ba.Ca.144-163].
1832. NDA, IHR.
1837, 1841. BLN, IHR.
1847. var. NDA, BLN, IHR.
1852. var's. NDA, BLN, IHR.
1854*, 1857. NDA, IHR.
1859. IHR, Yale UL.
1863*. NDA, IHR.
1865. var. NDA, BLN, IHR.
1868. var. NDA, BLN, IHR.

Devon continued
Exeter
See M.G. Smith, 'The Cathedral Chapter of Exeter and the election of 1705: a reconsideration', *Trans. Devonshire Association* **116** (1984).
1761. Cornwall RO, IHR, House of Lords RO (defective).
1776*, 1784. ECL, IHR.
1790. ECL, Bod, IHR.
1802. ECL, IHR, SoG.
1816. GL (in copy with 1818).
1818. var. ECL, Bod, GL, IHR, SoG.
1831. ECL, GL, IHR.
1835. ECL, IHR.
1845*. DRO, IHR.
1852, 1864*. ECL, IHR.
1868. ECL, IHR, Manchester UL.

Honiton
1763*. GL (copy).

Okehampton
1802. Bod [MS Eng. Misc. C.111].

Plymouth
1739. WDRO [710/727].
1780. WDRO [W92].
1806-59. WDRO [88/20-21].
1852, 1853*. ECL (published together), IHR.

Totnes
1812, 1837, 1839*, 1840*, 1857, 1859, 1865. Totnes Community Archive, IHR.
Sims shows **1812, 1837** and **1859** as being at DRO, but they cannot be located.

DORSET

Abbreviations (national collections, page 14)
DRO = Dorset Record Office.
DCL = Dorchester Central Library.
LRM = Lyme Regis Museum.
PCL = Poole Central Library; many holdings are photocopies.
WCL = Weymouth Central Library.

Constituency histories: Seaton (1986), page 12.

County
1726/7*. DRO, WCL, IHR.
1806. DRO (Blandford and Sherborne Divisions only); WCL, IHR.
1807. DRO (Blandford and Sturminster Divisions, and Cerne Sub-division only); BL, Bod, GL, IHR, SoG. Available as Microfiche 5 from SoG.
1831. DCL, WCL, GL, SoG.
1831*. Bod, GL, IHR, DRO; also DRO (Sherborne only).
1857. DCL, WCL, Bod, GL, SoG (incl. refs. to 1831, 1857). See C. Harvey,'The Dorset county election of 1857', *Dorset Nat. Hist. & Arch. Soc. Proc.* **98** (1976).

Dorset continued
Bridport
1795, 1796, 1802, 1806, 1812, 1820, 1832, 1835. DRO.
1841, 1847. DRO, IHR.
1859. var. DRO, BLN, IHR, Yale UL.

Dorchester
1705, 1752, 1762, 1774, 1780, 1790. DRO.

Lyme Regis
1837, 1841. LRM.
1859. Present location unavailable.
1865. DRO, IHR.

Poole
1698. PCL.
1790. PCL.
1796, 1801, 1802, 1806. PCL ('no poll necessary').
1807. PCL.
1808, 1812, 1818, 1820. PCL ('no poll necessary' or 'unused').
1826. PCL.
1828-34. Series of 27 poll books for elections of various local government officials: Mayor, coroner, sheriff, recorder etc., PCL.
1831. PCL.
1835. PCL, GL.
1835*. PCL.
1837. Present location unavailable.
1841, 1847, 1850*, 1857. PCL, BL, IHR.
1859, 1865. PCL, IHR.

Shaftesbury
1679. DRO (copy).
1830. GL.

Wareham
1689, 1702. DRO.
1722. var. DRO ("unofficial').
1727. DRO.
1734. var. DRO.
1744. DRO.
1747, 1754. DRO ('unofficial').
1789. DRO.

Weymouth and Melcombe Regis
1727. DRO, IHR.
1813. DRO [D.1/JC 3].
1818. WCL.
1847. WCL, IHR.
1851 (municipal election). WCL.
1852. IHR, SoG.

County DURHAM

Abbreviations (national collections, page 14)
DCL = Darlington Central Library.
DCoL = Durham County Library.
DPD = Dept. of Palaeography and Diplomatic, University of Durham.
DRO = Durham County Record Office (publ. and unpubl. not differentiated).
DUL = Durham University Library.
GCL = Gateshead Central Library.
MUL = Manchester University Library.
NCL = Newcastle upon Tyne Central Library.
NRO = Northumberland Record Office.
SCL = Sunderland Central Library.

Constituency histories: Seaton (1986), page 12.
H.R. Kleineberger, *Durham elections: a list of material relating to Parliamentary elections in Durham, 1675-1874* (1956).

County
1675. GCL, GL (copy).
1679. GL (copy).
c.1760/1. Canvassers' notes: DPD [Baker Baker III 11/22,23-d,24,31a-d,32,33,34].
1761. DPD, DUL, NRO, Bod, GL, IHR; SoG (index to non-resident voters only).
1766. Canvasser's list: DPD [B.B. 12/63].
1790. DCoL, NCL, NRO, BL, GL, IHR, SoG.
1820. DCoL, DPD, GCL, NCL, SCL, Bod, IHR, MUL, SoG.

North Co. Durham
1832. DCoL, DPD, GCL, NCL, SCL, BL, GL, IHR, MUL, SoG.
1837. var. DCoL, DPD, SCL, BL, Bod, GL, MUL.
1865. DCoL, DUL, GCL, NCL, IHR.
1868. var. DCoL, GCL, NCL, NRO, South Shields CL, SCL, BL, Bod, CUL, MUL, SoG.

South Co. Durham
1832. DCoL, DPD, NCL, Bod, GL, MUL, SoG.
1841. DCoL, SCL, BL, GL, IHR.
1857. NCL, IHR.
1865. DCoL, GCL, IHR.
1868. var. DCoL, NRO, BL, Bod, CUL, MUL, IHR.

Darlington
1862. Local Board of Health only: DCoL, Darlington RO [D/DL/22/8].
c.1866. Voters objected to only: DCoL.
1868. DCoL, IHR.

Durham City
1678. GL (copy).
1761. DPD, DRO, SCL, Bod, CUL, GL.
1761*. DPD, SCL, Bod, GL, IHR, SoG.
1774. var. DUL, GL.
1800*. var. DCoL, DPD, SCL, Bod, GL, IHR.
1802. var. DPD, NCL, NRO, SCL, BL, Bod, GL, IHR, Manchester CL.
1804*. DPD, DUL, IHR.
1813. DRO [D/Lo/F1019].

Durham City continued
1813*. DUL, NCL, SCL, Bod, GL, IHR, SoG.
1818. Election agent's book: DPD [Durham City Guild Records: Masons/5].
1830. var. DCoL, DPD, DRO, NCL, SCL, Bod, GL, IHR, MUL, SoG.
1831*. DCoL, DPD, NCL, SCL, Bod, GL, IHR.
1832. DCoL, DPD, DRO, NCL, SCL, Bod, GL, MUL, SoG.
1835. DPD, DRO, DUL, IHR.
1837. DCoL, DPD, DRO, NCL, SCL, Bod, GL, MUL, SoG.
1843 April*. DPD, DRO, DUL, NCL, SCL, GL.
1843 July*. DCoL, DPD, DRO, NCL, GL, IHR, SoG.
1847. DPD, DUL, NCL, SCL, GL.
1852. DPD, DRO, DUL, SCL, IHR, SoG.
1852*. DUL, NCL, IHR.
1853*. DRO (part only); DCoL, DUL, IHR.
1868. DRO (part only); DCoL, IHR.
1871*. DCoL, DUL, NCL, IHR, SoG.

Gateshead
1837. GCL, NCL, Tyne & Wear Archives Service (Newcastle), IHR.
1846-1872. Local elections only: GCL.
1852. GCL, NCL, IHR.

Hartlepools
1868. BLN, IHR.

South Shields
1832. GL.
1852. Tynemouth CL, GL.

Stockton on Tees
1868. South Shields CL, SCL, Stockton Ref. Lib., GL, IHR, SoG.

Sunderland
1761. Canvasser's list: DPD [B.B. 12/62].
1832. SCL, GL.
1833. NCL, IHR.
1837. SCL, GL.
1841*. SCL, GL.
1845*. BLN, IHR.
1847. DPD, BLN, IHR.
1847*. BLN, IHR.
1852. var. BLN, IHR.
1855*, 1857. BLN, IHR.
1859. BL.
1865, 1866*. BLN, IHR.

ESSEX

Abbreviations (national collections, page 14)
CoCL = Colchester Central Library.
CoRO = Essex Record Office (Colchester & N.E. Essex Branch).
EAS = Essex Archaeological Society.
ERO = Essex Record Office (Chelmsford).
GCL = Grays Central Library.
SCL = Southend Central Library.
WFL = Waltham Forest Archive & Local History Library.

Constituency histories: Seaton (1986), page 12.

County
1679. ERO [D/DKw 04].
1694*. CoCL, ERO, IHR, SoG.
1702. GL.
1710. ERO, Bod, IHR, GL; SoG (index to non-resident voters only).
1715*. ERO, Bod, IHR.
1722. CoCL, IHR.
1734. SoG ('Freeholders' book').
1734. ERO, WFL, BL, Bod, CUL, GL, IHR, Manchester UL; SoG (index to non-resident voters only).
1763*. var. ERO, WFL, BL, Bod, GL, IHR, SoG.
1768. ERO, WFL, BL, Bod, IHR, SoG.
1774. CoCL, ERO, WFL, Bod, GL, IHR.
1810*. ERO, WFL, Bod, GL, SoG.
1812. CoCL, ERO; GL (has 1810 poll also).
1830*. CoCL, ERO, WFL, Bod, GL, IHR, SoG.
1831. ERO, IHR.

East Essex
1868. ERO, GL, IHR.

North Essex
1832 (electoral register with MS poll forms attached) ERO, IHR.
1847. ERO, IHR.
1865. WFL, IHR.

South Essex
n.d. SCL.
1832. IHR.
1835-7(?), *1841* (all MS poll forms). ERO.
1857. ERO, BL, Bod, IHR.
1859. ERO, GCL, WFL, IHR.
1865. ERO, IHR.

Colchester
See J. Round, *A collection of poll books for Colchester (1741-1820)*.
1741. var. CoCL, EAS, IHR, SoG.
1747. CoCL, IHR, SoG.
1768. CoCL, Bod, IHR.
1780. ERO (part only) [D/DQs 108].
1780. CoCL, ERO, IHR.
1781*. var's. CoCL, GL, EAS, IHR.
1784. var. CoCL, EAS, ERO, Bod, IHR.
1784*. CoCL, Bod, IHR.
1788*. var. CoCL, EAS, IHR.

Colchester continued
1790. CoCL, Bod, GL, IHR.
1796. CoCL, Bod, IHR.
1806. var. CoCL, ERO, Bod, IHR.
1807. CoCL, Bod, IHR.
1812. CoCL, ERO, WFL, BL, GL, IHR.
1813. Election of Recorder: GL.
1818*. CoCL, IHR.
1818. CoCL, GL, IHR.
1819. Election of Recorder: BL.
1820. CoRO [Acc.C1].
1820. CoCL, ERO, BL, GL, IHR.
1821. Council election: CoCL, GL.
1830. CoRO [Acc.C1].
1830. CoCL, ERO, IHR, SoG.
1831. CoRO [Acc.C1].
1831*. CoCL, ERO, BL, GL, IHR.
1831. var. CoCL, EAS, IHR.
1832. CoRO [Acc.C1].
1832. CoCL, ERO, IHR.
1832*. CoCL.
1832. Council election: CoCL.
1835. CoCL, ERO, GL, IHR.
1835, 1836. Council elections: CoCL.
1837. CoRO [Acc.C1].
1837. CoCL, ERO, IHR.
1842. Council election: CoCL.
1843. Election of Councillor: GL.
1847. CoCL, ERO, GL, IHR.
1849 Council election: ERO, GL.
1850*. CoCL, WFL, IHR.
1852. var. CoCL, IHR.
1857*. CoCL, BLN, IHR.
1857, 1859. BLN, IHR.
1865. var's. ERO, CoCL, IHR.
1867*, 1868, 1870*. CoCL, IHR.

Harwich
1857. ERO, IHR.
1859. IHR, Yale UL.

Leyton
1875, 1876. Urban Sanitary District only: WFL.

Maldon
1761. ERO, IHR.
1787. ERO [D/DQs 136/1].
1807. ERO, IHR.
1826. ERO, WFL, BL, Bod, CUL, GL, IHR, SoG.
1837. ERO (incomplete 1836 electoral register with MS note of 1837 poll).
1841. GCL, BL, IHR.
1847, 1852. ERO, GCL, BL, IHR.
1857. BL, IHR, Liverpool RO.
1859. ERO, GCL, IHR.
1865. ERO, IHR.

GLOUCESTERSHIRE and BRISTOL

Abbreviations (national collections, page 14)
BCL = Bristol Central Library (MS copies in the Local History library require 24 hours' notice).
BRO = Bristol Record Office.
CCL = Cirencester Central Library.
GCL = Gloucester Central Library.
GRO = Gloucestershire Record Office.

Constituency histories: Seaton (1986), page 12.

County
1706. Index to non-resident voters: SoG (location of original unknown).
1710 (Langley and Swineshead Hundred only) BCL [Ellacombe MSS: Bitton, Oldham and Hanham vol.]; printed in 'Gloucestershire Voters in 1710' by C. Roy Hudlestone, *Bristol & Glouc. Arch. Soc. Trans.* **58** (1936), offprint SoG.
1714/5. GL.
1734. GRO [D674a X3].
1763, 1768, 1776. GRO [Q/Rep 1, 2, 3].
1776*. var. GCL, BL, Bod, GL, IHR, Nat. Lib. Wales; SoG (also index to non-resident voters).
1789. GRO [Q/Rep 4].
1811*. BRO, GCL, GRO, BL, Bod, GL.

East Gloucestershire
1832. GRO [Q/Rep 5].
1832. GCL, IHR.
1834. GRO [Q/Rep 7].
1834*. GCL, Bod, IHR.
1854*. GCL, GRO, Bod, IHR.

West Gloucestershire
1832. GRO [Q/Rep 6].

Bristol
1715. IHR, BRO, GL, SoG, College of Arms; voters in St. Augustine the Less reprinted in *Bristol & Glos. Arch. Soc. Record Branch* **3** (1956)
1722. BCL, RL, BRO, Dristol Museum, GL, IHR; SoG (also index to non-resident voters); (1722 poll book reprinted 1899).
1734. var. BCL, BRO, BL, Bod, GL, IHR.
1739*. BCL, BRO, IHR.
1754. var's. BCL, BRO, BL, GL, IHR; SoG (also index of non-resident voters).
1774. var. BCL, BRO, GL, IHR, SoG.
1781*. BCL, BRO, BL, GL, IHR, SoG.
1784. BCL, BRO, IHR.
1812. BCL, BRO, BL, GL, IHR, SoG.
1818. BRO.
1820. BCL, BRO.
1830. BCL, BRO, GL, IHR, SoG.
1832. var. BCL, BRO, GL, IHR, Manchester UL, SoG.
1835. BCL, BRO, GL, SoG.
1835. Council election: BCL.
1837. var. BCL, BRO, BL, Bod, GL, IHR, SoG.
1841. BCL, BRO, GL, IHR, SoG.
1847. var. BCL, BRO, IHR, SoG.
1852. BCL, GL, IHR.

Cheltenham
1841, 1847, 1848*. GCL, IHR.
1852. var. GCL, IHR, SoG.
1856*. GCL, IHR.
1859. GCL, IHR, SoG.
1865. var. GCL, IHR, Manchester UL.
1868. GCL, IHR.

Cirencester
1768. GCL, GRO, IHR.
1790. GCL, IHR.
1802. var. CCL, GCL, GL, IHR.
1812. CCL, GCL, IHR.
1848*. CCL, IHR.
1852. CCL, Bod, IHR.
1857. var. CCL, GCL, GRO, Bod, IHR.
1859. var. CCL, GCL, IHR.
1865. var's. CCL, GCL, Bod, IHR.
1868. var's. CCL, GCL, IHR.

Gloucester
1741. GCL, IHR.
1816*. var. GCL, BL, IHR.
1818. var. GCL, GL, IHR, SoG.
1830. var. GCL, GL, IHR, Bristol & Glouc. Arch. Soc.
1832, 1833*. GCL, IHR.
1835. GCL, GRO, IHR.
1837, 1838*, 1841. GCL, IHR.
1852. GCL, GRO, IHR.
1853*, 1857, 1859, 1862*. GCL, IHR.
1865. GCL, IHR, SoG.
1868. GCL, IHR.

Stroud
1832. GCL, IHR.
1841. var. GCL, IHR.
1852. GCL, GRO, IHR.
1867*. BLN, IHR.
1868. GCL, GRO, IHR.

Tewkesbury
1797. GRO [D1610 X17].
1831. GCL, GRO, GL.
1832. GRO [TBR A8/1].
1832, 1835. GCL, GRO, GL.
1837, 1841. GCL, GL.
1851/2. Canvass books: GRO [D2079/1/74].
1852. BL.
1865, 1868. GRO.

HAMPSHIRE

Abbreviations (national collections, page 14)
CCM = Carisbrooke Castle Museum, Isle of Wight.
HRO = Hampshire Record Office.
IWRO = Isle of Wight Record Office.
PCRO = Portsmouth City Records Office.
SCL = Southampton Central Library.
SRO = Southampton Record Office.
SUL = Southampton University Library.
WCL = Winchester City Library.

Constituency histories: Seaton (1986), page 12.

County
1705. SUL, IWRO, IHR; BL (MS transcript [L.R.33 a17]).
1710. Bod, IHR.
1713. HRO, IWRO, BL, Bod, IHR.
1734. IWRO, WCL, GL.
1779*. HRO, IWRO (Isle of Wight voters only), Bod, GL.
1790. HRO, IWRO, Bod, GL, IHR, SoG.
1806. HRO, GL, IHR.
1807. SUL, GL, IHR.

North Hampshire
1857. HRO (Basingstoke district only [8M62/183]).
1865. HRO (Basingstoke and Kingsclere districts [8M62/183]; Petersfield district [4M51/393]).

South Hampshire
1835. HRO (Ringwood only [12M60/91]).

Andover
1727, 1761. HRO [20M50/15,16].
1859, 1863*. BLN, IHR.

Christchurch
1727. HRO, SUL, Bod, IHR.

Isle of Wight County
1832. CCM, IHR.
1835. IHR.
1847. Canvass book (?): GL.
1852. Present location unavailable.
1857. IWRO, IHR.
1859. Present location unavailable.
1865, 1870. IWRO, IHR.

Lymington
1859. IHR, Yale UL.

Newport
1832. CCM, IHR.
1835. IWRO [NBC/45/215].
1835. IWRO, IHR.
1837. IWRO (Newport, Northwood, Whippingham, Carisbrooke and St. Nicholas voters only [NBC/45/216-18]).
1840*. IWRO (Newport voters only [NBC/45/219]).
1841. IWRO (Carisbrooke, St. Nicholas, Northwood and Whippingham voters only [NBC/45/220-21]).
1841. CCM, IHR.
1847. IWRO. IHR.
1852. BL.

Newport continued
1857*. IWRO, CCM, IHR.
1859. Present location unavailable.
1865. IWRO, IHR.

Petersfield
1830. Poll book or canvass book (?): GL.
1832. HRO [20M50/111]; Somerset RO [H. Jolliffe papers].

Portsea
1833-35. PCRO [among registers of electors, V 1/1,3].

Portsmouth
1681. HRO [5M50/1610].
1713, 1714. PCRO [copies, PE 7].
1741, 1774, 1777, 1780. PCRO [PE 2].
1790. Canvass of freeholders: PCRO [PE 9].
1820. PCRO [PE 6].
1834/5. PCRO [among register of electors, V 1/3].
1835. BLN, IHR.

Southampton
1727. SRO.
1734. HRO [4M78/Z6]; SRO.
1734. HRO.
1737, 1741. SRO.
1741. BL [1509/1501: 'Town & County of Southampton'].
1774. SRO.
1774. SUL, IHR.
1790. var's. SCL, SRO, SUL, GL, IHR.
1794*. var. SCL, SRO, SUL, IHR.
1802. SCL, SUL, IHR.
1806. SRO, GL.
1806. var. SCL, SUL, IHR.
1812. var. SCL, SRO, SUL, IHR.
1818. var. SCL, SUL, IHR.
1820. SRO.
1820. var. HRO, SCL, SUL, IHR.
1830. SRO.
1830. SCL, IHR.
1831. SRO.
1831. var. SUL, IHR.
1832. SRO.
1832. SCL, SUL, IHR.
1835. SRO.
1835. HRO, SUL, IHR.
n.d., prob. *1837.* SRO.
1837. HRO, SCL, SUL, IHR.
1841. var. SCL, SRO, SUL, IHR.
1842*. SCL, SRO, SUL, IHR.
1852. var. HRO, SCL, SRO, BL, IHR.
1852, 1853. Inspector's and clerk's poll books: SRO.
1857*. BLN, IHR.
1865. SCL, GL.

Winchester
1715. HRO [W/B9/2/6].
1734. HRO [W/K5/3 fo.65b].
1835. var. HRO, WCL, BL, IHR.
1837. var. HRO, WCL, IHR.

Hampshire: *Winchester* continued
1841. HRO, IHR.
1847. WCL, BL, IHR.
1852. var. HRO, WCL, BL, IHR.
1857. WCL, IHR.
1859. var. HRO, WCL, IHR.
1865. HRO [W/B9/2/29-30].
1865. HRO, WCL, IHR.
1868. var. HRO, WCL, IHR.

HEREFORDSHIRE
(now part of Hereford & Worcester)

Abbreviations (national collections, page 14)
HCL = Hereford City Library.
HRO = Hereford & Worcester Record Office, Hereford.
NLW = National Library of Wales, Aberystwyth.

Constituency histories: Seaton (1986), page 12.

County
1722. HCL, GL, NLW.
1754. HCL, BL, IHR, NLW.
1774. HCL, BL, GL, NLW.
1796. HCL, BL, Bod, GL, NLW, SoG.
1802. HCL, HRO, BL, Bod, IHR, NLW, SoG.
1818. HCL, HRO, BL, GL, IHR, NLW, SoG.
1835. HCL, HRO, IHR.
1837, 1841, 1842*. HRO.
1852. HCL, HRO, Bod, GL, IHR, NLW, SoG.
1857, 1868. HCL, HRO, Bod, GL, IHR, SoG.

Hereford
1741. HCL, Bod, GL, IHR, NLW.
1747, 1754. HCL, IHR.
1761. HCL, Bl , IHR, NLW.
1818. var. HCL, HRO, BL, GL, IHR, NLW, SoG.
1826. var. HCL, HRO, Bod, IHR, SoG.
1832. HCL, IHR, SoG.
1835. HCL, HRO, IHR, SoG. Reprinted in *Herefordshire FHS Journal*, 2.10 (Summer 1985).
1837. HCL, HRO, IHR.
1841, 1841*, 1852, 1865, 1868, 1869*, 1871*. HCL, IHR.

Leominster
1741. BL.
1742*. NLW, IHR.
1796. HCL, IHR, NLW, SoG.
1797*. HCL, HRO, GL.
1802, 1812, 1818, 1820, 1826, 1831. HCL, IHR.
1837, 1852. HCL, HRO, IHR.
1868. HCL, IHR.

HERTFORDSHIRE

Abbreviations (national collections, page 14)
ERO = Essex Record Office, Chelmsford.
HRO = Hertfordshire Record Office.
HLS = Hertfordshire Local Studies Collection.
SAL = St. Albans Central Library

Constituency histories: Seaton (1986), page 12.

County
1697. HRO [QPE.1-3].
1705. IHR, SoG.
1708. HRO [D/EX.294 Z.1].
1714. HRO [QPE.5; also 18809, incomplete].
1722. HRO [QPE.6-12].
1722. HRO, IHR.
1727. HRO [QPE.14-20].
1727. HRO, BL, ERO, Bod, GL, IHR, SoG.
1734. HRO [QPE.22-31].
1734. HRO, HLS, BL, ERO, Bod, GL, IHR, SoG.
1736. HRO [QPE.32-38; also D/EH.1 F.137, copy].
1754. HRO [QPE.39-62; also 51159-61, incomplete].
1754. HRO, HLS, BL, Bod, GL, IHR; SoG (also index to non-resident voters).
1761. HRO [QPE.63-87A].
1761. HLS, ERO, Bod, GL, IHR; SoG (index to non-resident voters only).
1774. HRO [QPE.88-111; 112-131. Two sets].
1774. HRO, HLS, BL, Bod, GL, IHR, Manchester UL; SoG (also index to non-resident voters).
1784. HLS, HRO, SAL, BL, Bod, GL, IHR; SoG (also index to non-resident voters).
1790. HRO [QPE.132-151].
1790. HRO, BL, Bod, GL, IHR; SoG (also index to non-resident voters).
1796. HRO [QPE.152-167].
1796. HRO, SAL, Bod, GL; SoG (index to non-resident voters only).
1802. HRO [QPE.168-182].
1802. SAL, IHR, BL, Bod, GL, Cambs. R.O. (Huntingdon branch), Manchester UL; SoG (also index to non-resident voters).
1805*. HRO [QPE.183-201; also D/EX.582 Z.1, out-county voters only].
1805*. HRO, SAL, BL, ERO, Bod, GL, IHR, SoG.
1818. HRO (St Albans county voters only) [QPE.87B].
1832. SoG (Electoral register with MS poll added).
1832. HRO, Bod, GL, Watford CL.
1833. SAL.

Hertford
1727. HRO [D/EPF.273].
1831. Present location unavailable.
1835. IHR, SoG.
1837. HRO [in *County Press* 5 Aug. 1837], IHR.
1852. HRO [QPE.201A, from county election].
1852. HLS, IHR.
1857. HLS, HRO, IHR.
1859. HLS, IHR.
1868. HRO, IHR.

Hertfordshire continued
St. Albans
1780. HRO [D/ER.401]
1807. Bod, IHR.
1812. HRO [D/EHR F.139].
1820, 1821*, 1830, 1831. SAL, IHR.
1832. var. HRO, SAL, IHR.
1835. HRO, SAL, IHR.
1837. SAL, IHR.
1841*. SAL, IHR.
1847. BL, IHR.

HUNTINGDONSHIRE
Now part of Cambridgeshire.

Abbreviations (national collections, page 14)
HDL = Huntingdon Divisional Library.
HRO = Huntingdon Branch, Cambridgeshire County Record Office. Photocopies of all **County** poll books are available on the search room shelves. Those **1826-59** include indexes of names.
NM = Norris Museum, St. Ives.
PMS = Peterborough Museum Society Library.

Constituency histories: Seaton (1986), page 12.
Dr P. Saunders, 'Huntingdonshire Poll Books and Electoral Registers to 1900', *Huntsman* (Hunts. FHS) **1**.8 (October 1989).

County
1710, 1713. Bod [MS. Gough Hunts. 3]; photocopies: HRO, NM.
1768. HRO, NM, PMS, BL, Bod, IHR.
1790. HRO [HINCH 8/2, later used for canvassing].
1807. HDL, HRO, NM, GL, IHR, SoG.
1818. HDL, HRO, NM, BL, Bod, CUL, GL, SoG.
1826. HDL, HRO, NM, BL, Bod, CUL, GL, IHR, SoG.
1830. HDL, HRO, NM, PMS, IHR.
1831. HRO, NM, BL, GL.
1837. HDL, HRO, NM, PMS, GL.
1857. HDL, HRO, NM, PMS, BL, Bod, CUL, GL, IHR.
1859. HDL, HRO, NM, PMS, GL, SoG.

Huntingdon
1702. HRO [H.26/19].
1741. HRO (19th century copy) [Acc 857:SM.24/474].
1824. HRO [H.4 and HINCH 8/190].
1831. HRO.
1832. HRO [HINCH 8/187/2, an annotated electoral register].
1832. GL, IHR; HRO (copy).

KENT
Abbreviations (national collections, page 14)
AL = Ashford Library.
BLHL = Bexley Local History Library.
BCL = Bromley Central Library.
CCL = Canterbury Central Library.
CRL = Chatham Reference Library.
DaL = Dartford Central Library.
DeL = Deal Library.
DoL = Dover Library.
GCL = Gillingham Central Library.
GdCL = Gravesend Central Library.
GLL = Greenwich Local History Library.
HGS = Institute of Heraldic and Genealogical Studies, Canterbury.
KAO = Kent Archives Office, Maidstone
KFHS Mf = Issued on microfiche by the Kent Family History Society (available from John Douch, 33 Castle St., Dover, Kent CT16 1PT). A complete set is at Maidstone Library.
KUL = Library, University of Kent at Canterbury.
ML = Maidstone Library.
MgL = Margate Central Library.
MUL = Manchester University Library.
OBL = Orpington Branch Library.
PBL = Penge Branch Library.
RgL = Ramsgate Library.
RL = Rochester Library.
SL = Sevenoaks Library.
TWL = Tunbridge Wells Library.
WCL = Woolwich Central Library.

Constituency histories: Seaton (1986), page 12.
W.F. Bergess and B.R.M. Riddell, *Kent Directories Located*, Kent County Library (1978) (includes poll books and electoral registers);
D.S. Cousins, 'Poll books - how Fordwich voted in Parliamentary elections (County and East Kent)', in K.M. McIntosh (ed.), *Fordwich: the lost port* (1975).
D. Harrington, 'Poll Books', *Kent FH*, **5**.1 (Dec. '86).

County
1640. Bod [Top. Kent e.6]. See F.W. Jessup, 'The Kentish election of March 1640', *Arch. Cant.* **86** (1971).
1713. KAO [U.269/O 104/1, Q/RPe 1].
1714, 1722. KAO [Q/RPe 1].
1727. KAO [Q/RPe 1, U.269/O 104/2].
1727. Canvass lists: KAO [U.269/O 105/1-2].
1734. KFHS Mf.184; AL (MF), BLHL, CCL, CRL, DaL, DeL, DoL, GLL, HGS (MF), KAO, MgL, RgL, SL, TWL, Bod, GL, ML, MUL, IHR, SoG.
1743. SoG (index to non-resident voters only).
1747. KAO [MS No U.1592 04]; CCL (copy).
1753/4. Canvass lists: KAO [U.269/O 105/3]; Sevenoaks only [U.269/O 105/5].
n.d. Canvass lists: KAO [U.269/O 105/4].
1754. KAO [Q/RPe 1].
1754. KFHS Mf.185; AL (MF); BLHL, CCL, DaL (MF), DoL, GLL, HGS (MF), KAO, ML, RgL, BL, Bod, GL, IHR, SoG.

Kent: County continued

1790. KAO [Q/RPe 1], also Canvass list (Sevenoaks only) [U.269/0146]; CCL.
1790. KFHS Mf.186; AL, BLHL, CCL, CRL, DeL, DaL, DoL, GCL, GdCL, GLL, HGS (MF), KAO, KUL, ML, MUL, RgL, RL, TWL, BL, Bod, CUL, GL, IHR, SoG.
1796, 1802. KAO [Q/RPe 1].
1802. KFHS Mf.187; AL, BLHL, CCL, CRL, DaL, DoL, GdCL, GLL, HGS (MF), KAO, KUL, ML, MUL, RgL, RL, BL, Bod, GL, IHR, SoG.
1806. KAO [Q/RPe 1].
1810(?). KAO [Q/RPe 1] (no date on MS).
1818. KAO [Q/RPe 1].
1832, 1835. KAO [Q/RPe 1].

East Kent
See M. Drake, 'The Mid-Victorian voter', *Journal of Interdisciplinary History* **1**, 3 (Spring 1971).
D.S. Cousins, 'Vote for Dering?', in K.H. McIntosh (ed.), *Hoath and Herne: the last of the forest* (1984).
1832. KFHS Mf.193; AL (MF), CCL, DoL, HGS (MF), MgL, ML, KAO, KUL, MUL, RgL, BL, GL, IHR, SoG.
1837. KAO [Q/RPe 1]; and another for this Division, n.d. [U.795/01].
1837. KFHS Mf.192; AL, CCL, CRL, DoL, GLL, HGS (MF), KUL, ML, RgL, BL, Bod, IHR, MUL, SoG.
1852*. DoL, KAO, KUL, RgL, Bod, GL, SoG.
1852. KFHS Mf.193; AL, CCL, DeL, GCL, GLL, HGS (MF), KUL, RgL, BL, GL, IHR, MUL, SoG.
1857. KFHS Mf.188; AL (MF), CCL, DeL, DoL, GCL, GLL, HGS (MF), KAO, KUL, RgL, Bod, IHR, SoG (MF).
1863*. KFHS Mf.189; AL, CCL, CRL, DeL, DoL, GLL, HGS (MF), KAO, KUL, MgL, RgL, Bod, CUL, GL, IHR, MUL, SoG.
1865. var. KFHS Mf.190; AL, BLHL, CCL, DoL, GCL, GLL, HGS, KAO, KUL, RgL, ML, Bod, GL, IHR, MUL, SoG, Folkestone CL.
1868*. GCL, KAO, MgL, ML, RgL, GL.
1868. KFHS Mf.191; AL (MF), CCL, DeL, DoL, GCL, HGS (MF), KUL, MgL, ML, RgL, GL, IHR, SoG.

Mid-Kent
1868. DoL, GL.

West Kent
1832. GL (Cranbrook district only).
1835. AL, BLHL, BCL, CRL, DaL (MF), DoL, GdCL, GCL, GLL, HGS, KAO, KUL, ML, SL, TWL, BL, Bod, GL, IHR, SoG.
1836. PBL.
1837. KAO [Q/RPe 1].
1837. AL (MF), BCL, BLHL, CRL, DaL, DoL, GCL, GLL, KAO, KUL, ML, MUL, RL, SL, BL, Bod, GL, IHR, SoG, Hastings CL.
1847. AL, BCL, BLHL, DaL (MF), DoL, GCL, GLL, HGS, KAO, ML, OBL, PBL, RL, SL, BL, Bod, GL, GL, IHR, MUL, SoG, Greater London History Library.

West Kent continued
1852. KFHS Mf; AL (MF), BCL, BLHL, CRL, DaL, DoL, GdCL, GLL, KAO, KUL, ML, PBL, RL, BL, Bod, CUL, GL, IHR, MUL, SoG.
1857*. var. ML, RgL, Bod, IHR, SoG.
1857. var. KFHS Mf; AL (MF), BLHL, CRL, DaL, DoL, GdCL, GCL, GLL, HGS, KAO, KUL, ML, RgL, RL, Bod, GL, IHR, MUL, SoG.
1859. KFHS Mf; AL (MF), BLHL, CRL, GLL, KAO, ML, OBL, RgL, RL, Bod, GL, IHR.
1865. AL (MF), CRL, DaL, DoL, GCL, GdCL, GLL, HGS, KAO, KUL, ML, OBL, RL, SL, BL, Bod, GL, IHR, MUL, SoG.
1868. AL (MF), DoL, GdCL, GLL, KAO, KUL, RL, Bod, GL, IHR, MUL, SoG.

Canterbury
1734. BL [Add. MS 28014]; KAO [Q/RPe 1, U.269/O 104/3]; CCL (MF).
1747. KAO [U.1592/04]; CCL (p'copy), GL.
1768. KFHS Mf.157; CCL (MF), HGS (MF), IHR.
1780. KFHS Mf.194; CCL (MF), HGS (MF), IHR, SoG (MF).
1790. KFHS Mf.195; CCL (MF), HGS (MF), IHR, SoG.
1794 (mayoral election). GLL.
1796. KFHS Mf 158; GLL, CCL, HGS (MF), BL, GL, IHR, SoG (MF).
1818. KFHS Mf.193; GLL, CCL, HGS (MF), BL, GL, IHR.
1826. CCL (copy), GLL, WCL, BL, IHR.
1830. KFHS Mf.193; GLL, CCL, HGS (MF), BL, Bod, GL, IHR, MUL, SoG.
1832. KFHS Mf.193; GLL, CCL, HGS (MF), GL, IHR.
1835. KFHS Mf.196; CCL, CRL, HGS (MF), KAO, BL, Bod, GL, IHR, MUL, SoG.
1835. Town Council elections: CCL, BL, GL, SoG.
1836. Town Council elections: CCL, BL, GL.
1837. var. KFHS Mf.107-0; GLL, CCL, HGS (MF), WCL, BL, IHR, SoG (MF).
1841*. KFHS Mf.198; GLL, CCL, HGS (MF), GL, IHR, SoG (MF).
1841. KFHS Mf.199; CCL, HGS (MF), WCL, IHR.
1847. var. KFHS Mf.200; GLL, CCL, GL, HGS (MF), WCL, GL, IHR, SoG (MF).
1852. KFHS Mf.201; CCL, GLL, HGS (MF), MCL, IHR, SoG (MF).
1854*. KFHS Mf.202; CCL, HGS (MF), MCL, BL, GL, SoG (MF).
1857. KFHS Mf.198; CCL, HGS (MF), WCL, BL, IHR, SoG (MF).
1862*. var. KFHS Mf.203; CCL, GLL, HGS (MF), MCL, WCL, IHR, SoG (MF).
1865. var. KFHS Mf.198; CCL, GLL, KAO, HGS (MF), IHR, SoG (MF).
1868. KFHS Mf.198; GLL, CCL, HGS (MF), IHR, SoG (MF).

Chatham
1832, 1834*. BL.
1852. BL.
1853*. MCL, BL, IHR.

Kent: *Chatham* continued
1857, 1859. GL.
1865. CRL, GL, IHR.
1868. CRL, IHR.

Deal (see also Sandwich)
1800-35. Elections of Mayor: KAO [De/RPb 1, 21 vols.].

Dover
1673. KAO [U.1015/3/30].
1741. Incomplete: KAO [U.1015/071].
1802. DoL.
1826. KFHS Mf 206; CCL, DoL, Bod, IHR.
1828*. DoL, Bod, IHR.
1830. GLL, DoL, Bod, GL, IHR, SoG.
1832, 1833*, 1835, 1837. DoL, Bod, GL, IHR.
1841. DoL, GL, IHR, SoG.
1847. DoL, GL, IHR.
1852. DoL, KAO, GL, IHR, SoG.
1857. DoL, GL, IHR.
1859. DoL, KAO, MCL, GL, IHR.
1865. DoL, GLL, GL, IHR, MUL.
1868. var. DoL, GLL, KAO, Bod, GL, IHR, MUL.
1871*. DoL, GLL, GL.

Folkestone
1820-35. Election of Chamberlain: KAO [AO.2/1-16].

Greenwich
1837. GLL, IHR.

Hythe
1802, 1807, 1810*, 1812, 1818, 1819*, 1830, 1832, 1837. GL.

Maidstone
1723*. ML.
1734. KAO, IHR.
1747. ML (typescript copy).
1761. ML, Bod, GL; SoG (index to non-resident voters only).
1768. ML, GL; SoG (index to non-resident voters only).
1774. ML, IHR.
1780. var. ML, Bod, IHR.
1784. ML, Bod, IHR.
1788*. ML, Bod, GL.
1790. ML, Bod, IHR.
1796. KAO.
1796. Bod.
1802. KAO, ML, Bod, IHR.
1806. ML, Bod, GL; SoG (index to non-resident voters only).
1807. ML, Bod, GL; SoG (also index to non-resident voters).
1812, 1818. ML, GL.
1820. GL, SoG.
1822. Council election: ML.
1826. var. ML, GL, IHR, SoG.
1826, 1830. Council elections: ML.
1830. var. ML, GL, IHR, SoG.
1831. ML, IHR.

Kent: *Maidstone* continued
1832. var. ML, IHR, SoG.
1835. ML, IHR.
1837. var. ML, GL, IHR.
1838*. KAO, ML, IHR.
1841, 1852. ML, IHR.
1853*. ML, BL, IHR.
1857. ML, IHR.
1859. ML, GL, IHR, SoG.
1865. var. ML, GL, IHR, SoG.
1868. ML. GL, SoG.
1870*. ML, GL, IHR.

Queenborough
1688, 1690, 1715 (3), **1722** (2), **1727** (2), **1728, 1747, 1754** (2), **1761, 1807** (2), **1810, 1826** (2). KAO [Qb/RPp].
1826. BL.

Rochester
1765, 1768. RL.
1768. BL, Bod, GL.
1771. RL
1771. Bod, GL.
1774. RL.
1774. BL.
1780. RL.
1780. BL, Bod, GL.
1784, 1790. RL.
1790. KAO. KUL, RL, BL, IHR.
1792. RL.
1792. BL.
1796. RL.
1802. RL, BL, Bod, GL, IHR, SoG. Published by NW Kent FHS (1989).
1806, 1807. RL, BL, Bod, GL, IHR, SoG.
1816*. var. GL, RL, BL.
1818. var. RL, BL, Bod, GL.
1826. RL, BL, GL.
1830. RL, BL, Bod, GL, IHR, SoG. Published by NW Kent FHS (1989).
1835. var. RL, GL, BL.
1837, 1841. RL, BL.
1847. RL, IHR.
1847*. RL.
1852. RL, BL, GL, IHR.
1856*. RL, GL, IHR.
1859. RL, BL, Bod, GL.
1865. RL, GL.
1868. RL, GL, IHR.

Sandwich (incl. Deal and Walmer)
n.d., c.1807. KAO [Sa/RPp 1,2].
1808. KAO.
1831. DeL, KAO, GL, IHR.
1831. Election of Rector of St. Peter's: KAO [SA/RPz 1].
1832. KAO, IHR.
1835. IHR, Sandwich Town Council Archives.
1837. KAO, IHR, SoG.

28

Kent: Sandwich continued
1840. Elections of Councillors, Auditors, Assessors: KAO [Sa/RPb 1-3].
1841*. BL.
1847, 1852. BL, GL.
1857. KAO, GL.
1859. GL.
1859*, 1865. IHR.
1868. DeL, GL.

LANCASHIRE

Abbreviations (national collections, page 14)
BCL = Bolton Central Library.
BRL = Blackburn Central Reference Library.
ByL = Bury Library and Arts Dept.
LaCL = Lancaster Central Library.
LCL = Liverpool Central Library.
LRO = Lancashire Record Office, Preston.
MCL = Manchester Central Library.
MUL = Manchester University Library.
OCL = Oldham Central Library.
PCL = Preston Central Library.
RCL = Rochdale Central Library.
WCL = Warrington Central Library.
WiCL = Wigan Central Library.
WiRO = Wigan Record Office, Leigh.

Constituency histories: Seaton (1986), page 12.

County
1700/1. LRO [DDK 1740/1].
(1722). See J.D. Alsop, 'Another eighteenth century election poll: Lancashire 1722', *Northern History* **17** (1981).
1772. LRO [DDLi box 91].

South Lancashire
1861. ByL (Townships of Bury, Elton, Heap, Pilkington, Pilsworth, Radcliffe, Tottington L.E. and H.E., Walmersley-cum-Shuttleworth, Bacup), IHR.

Ashton under Lyne
1841. IHR; Ashton CL (Tameside Local Studies) (copy).

Blackburn
1835. LRO, IHR.
1847. BLN, IHR.
1852. BLN, Bod, IHR.
1853*. BRL, BLN, IHR.
1865. BRL, GL.
1868. BRL (poll and canvass annotations on electoral register).

Lancashire continued
Bolton
1832. BCL, IHR.
1835. BCL, GL.
1837. BCL, IHR.
1841. BLN, IHR.
1847. BCL, LRO, IHR.
1849*. BLN, IHR.
1852. BCL. LRO, IHR.
1857. BLN, LRO, IHR.
1865. BCL, IHR.

Bury
1837, 1841. ByL, IHR.
1846 (local election). ByL.
1852, 1857, 1859. ByL, IHR.
1865. BLN, IHR.
1868. ByL, IHR.

Clitheroe
1640. LRO [DDX 28/83].
1628 and *1640.* Published in W.S. Weeks, *Clitheroe in the Seventeenth Century* (n.d.).
c.1661, 1713, 1727, 1747/8, 1780. LRO [MBC 162, 83, 732, 159, 736].
1853*. IHR, SoG.

Lancaster
(1660-1688). See M.A. Mullett, 'Conflict, politics and elections in Lancaster 1660-1688', *Northern History* **19** (1983).
1710. Draft: LRO [RCLn].
1768. LRO [DDCa 15/30].
1784. LaCL, LRO, BL, Bod, IHR.
1786*. LaCL, Bod, IHR.
1790. LaCL.
1802. LaCL, Bod, IHR.
1807, 1809. LaCL.
1818, 1837, 1841. LaCL, IHR.
1847. var. LaCL, LRO, IHR.
1848*. var. LaCL, IHR.
1852, 1853*, 1857, 1859, 1864*. LaCL, IHR.
1865. LaCL, MPL, IHR.

Liverpool
1734. LCL, IHR.
1761. var. LCL, LUL, Bod, GL, MCL.
1780. LCL, LRO, MCL, IHR, SoG.
1784. LCL, BL, Bod, IHR.
1790. LCL, Bod, GL, IHR, SoG.
1796. LCL, Bod, GL, IHR, MCL.
1802. var. LCL. BL, Bod, IHR.
1806. var's. LCL, LRO, BL, Bod, GL, MCL, IHR, SoG.
1807. LCL, GL, IHR.
1812. var. LCL, LRO, Bod, GL, IHR, MCL. See Jupp 1973.
1816*. MCL, BL, GL.
1818. LCL, BL, Bod, GL, IHR, MCL, SoG.
1820. LCL, IHR.
1827. Election of Mayor: GL.
1830*. var. LCL, BL, Bod, GL, IHR, MCL, SoG.

Lancashire: Liverpool continued
1832. LCL, BL, Bod, GL, IHR, MCL, MUL, SoG.
1835. LCL, BL, MUL, GL, IHR, SoG.
1835. Municipal election: LCL, BL, GL.
1837. LCL, BL, Bod, GL, IHR, MUL, SoG.
1840. Municipal election: LCL, GL.
1841. LUL, GL, IHR.
1841. Municipal election: BL.
1852. Present location unavailable.
1854. Municipal election: LCL.
1857. LCL, LRO, GL, IHR.

Manchester
1832. MCL, IHR, SoG.
1836. MCL (poll annotations on electoral register).
1839*. MCL, IHR.
1866. MCL (poll annotations on electoral register).

Oldham
1832. LRO [DDRe 14/1-2].
1832, 1835*, 1847. OCL, IHR.
1852. var. OCL, IHR.
1852*. var. OCL, IHR.
1857, 1859, 1865, 1868. OCL, IHR.

Preston
1727. LRO [DDPr 131/2a].
1741, 1768. LRO [DDKe 54].
1784, 1796. LRO [DDPr 131/10,11].
1807. PCL, LRO, MCL, Bod, GL, IHR, SoG.
1812. LRO, IHR, SoG.
1818. PCL, IHR, MCL.
1820. LRO, PCL, IHR, MCL.
1826. LRO [QDE 3]
1830*. var. LRO, PCL, MCL, IHR.
1832. PCL, IHR, MCL.
1835. LRO, IHR.
1837. LRO, PCL, IHR.
1841. var. LRO, PCL, MCL, IHR.
1847. PCL, IHR.
1852. LRO, PCL, MCL, IHR.
1857. LRO, IHR.
1859. LRO, PCL, IHR.
1862. LRO, IHR.
1868. PCL, GL.

Rochdale
1835. RCL, IHR.
1837*, 1841. RCL, IHR.
1852. RCL, IHR.
1857. var. RCL, IHR. See J.R. Vincent, 'The electoral sociology of Rochdale', *Econ. Hist. Review,* 11, xvi (1963), for an analysis of the **1841** and **1857** polls.

Salford
1841. MCL, IHR.

St. Helens
1855-63. Annual elections for Commissioners under the St. Helens Improvement Act of 1855: St. Helens Community Leisure Dept.

Warrington
1832, 1835. WCL, IHR.
1837. WCL.
1847. WCL, IHR.

Wigan
1628 and **1640** (2). Published in D. Sinclair, *History of Wigan,* 1882.
1768, 1820, 1830. WiRO.
1830. BL, Bod, GL.
1831, 1832, 1837. WiRo.
1837. BLN, IHR.
1841. WiRO.
1841. WiRO, IHR.
1845*. WiCL, WiRO, IHR.
1852. var's. WiCL, WiRO, IHR.
1854*. WiCL, WiRO, IHR.
1857. var. WiCL, WiRO, BLN, IHR.
1859. BLN, IHR.
1866*. WiCL, WiRO, IHR.

LEICESTERSHIRE

Abbreviations (national collections, page 14)
LCL = Leicester Central Library.
LL = Loughborough Library.
LRO = Leicestershire Record Office.
NUL = Nottingham University Library.

Constituency histories: Seaton (1986), page 12.

County
1715. LRO.
1719*. LCL, LL, LRO, BL, Bod, GL, IHR, SoG.
1741. LCL (indexed typescript); LRO, BL, Bod, GL, IHR, SoG. Available as Microfiche 009 from SoG.
1775. LRO.
1775*. var. LCL, LL, LRO, BL, Bod, CUL, GL, IHR, NUL; SoG (also index to non-resident voters).
1818. LRO.
1818. LCL, GL, SoG.
1830. var. LCL, LL, LRO, BL, Bod, GL, IHR, NUL, SoG, Derby CL.

North Leicestershire
1832. LCL, LRO, GL, IHR.
1841. GL.
1857. LCL, LRO, GL, SoG.
1859. LCL (copy); LRO, GL, IHR, SoG.
1865. LCL (copy); LRO, GL.

South Leicestershire
1841. LRO.
1841. var. LCL, LRO, Bod, GL, IHR, SoG.
1867*. LCL, LRO, Bod, GL, NUL, SoG.
1868, 1870*. LCL, GL.

Leicestershire continued
Leicester
1754. LCL, LRO, Bod, GL, IHR, SoG.
1768. var. GL, LCL, LRO, Bod, GL, IHR, Manchester UL, NUL; SoG (also index to non-resident voters).
1796. LCL, LRO, GL, IHR, SoG.
1800*. LCL, LRO, GL, IHR, NUL, SoG.
1826. var. LCL, LRO, BL, Bod, GL, IHR, NUL, SoG. See Anon. 'Lord Macaulay on the Leicester parliamentary election of 1826: "A New Song" ', *Leicestershire Historian* **2** (1980).
1832. var. LCL, LRO, Bod, GL, IHR, SoG.
1835. var. LCL, LRO, Bod, GL, IHR, SoG.
1837. var. LCL, Bod, IHR, NUL, SoG.
1839*. LCL, IHR.
1847. LCL, LRO, GL, IHR, SoG.
1852. LCL, LRO, BL, IHR.
1857. var. LCL, GL, SoG.
1859. LCL, GL.
1861*. LCL, GL, SoG.
1865. LCL, IHR.
1883. Election of Town Council, School Board, and Board of Guardians: LCL.

LINCOLNSHIRE

Abbreviations (national collections, page 14)
BCL = Boston Central Library.
EDL = Goulding Collection, East District Library HQ, Victoria Hall, Victoria Road, Louth.
GaL = Gainsborough Library.
GrL = Grantham Library.
GyL = Grimsby Central Library
HCL = Hull Central Library.
LAO = Lincolnshire Archives Office.
LCL = Lincoln Central Library.
MUL = Manchester University Library.
NUL = Nottingham University Library.
PDL = Peterborough Divisional Library.
PMS = Peterborough Museum Society Library.
SL = Sleaford Library.
STH = Stamford Town Hall.

Constituency histories: Seaton (1986), page 12.

County
1724*. LAO [Mon 7/41].
1724*. GyL, LAO, LCL, MUL, IHR.
1725*. GrL; Hyde Park FH Centre (MF).
1807. GyL, LAO, LCL, Bod, GL, IHR, SoG.
1818. GaL, GyL, LAO, LCL, SL, Bod, GL, IHR, MUL, NUL, PDL, PMS, SoG.
1823*. GaL, GyL, LAO, LCL, Bod, CUL, GL, IHR, MUL, NUL, PDL, PMS, SoG.

North Lincolnshire (Lindsey)
1832. GyL, LAO, LCL, Bod, GL.

Lincolnshire: *North Lincolnshire* continued
1835. GyL, LCL, Bod, GL, IHR.
1841. GaL, GyL, LAO, LCL, Bod, GL, HCL, IHR, MUL, SoG; NUL (part only).
1852. GaL, GyL, LAO, LCL, Bod, CUL, GL, HCL, IHR, MUL, NUL, PDL, PMS, SoG.

South Lincolnshire (Kesteven and Holland)
1832. LAO [Trollope papers].
1841. var. GyL, LAO, LCL, SL, Bod, GL, IHR, NUL, PMS, SoG.
1857. GyL, LAO, LCL, SL, Bod, GL, IHR, NUL, SoG.
1868. GyL, LAO, LCL, Bod, CUL, GL, MUL, NUL, SoG.

Boston
(1604-40). See J.K. Gruenfelder, 'Boston's early Stuart elections 1604-40', *Lincs. Hist. Arch.* **13** (1978).
1710. Univ. Coll. N. Wales (Dept. of MSS.), Bangor [Llig.828].
1796. NUL.
1802. GL, NUL; LCL copy in Sims not found.
1803. NUL.
1806. Bod, GL, NUL.
1807. IHR, NUL, Spalding Gentlemen's Society.
1812*. Bod, GL, NUL.
1812. Bod, IHR, NUL.
1818. var. LAO, LCL, GL, Bod, IHR, Manchester CL, NUL.
1820. var. LAO, GL, Bod, IHR.
1826. var. Bod, LAO, LCL, IHR.
1830. var. LCL, BL, GL, Bod, IHR.
1832, 1835, 1837. LCL, Bod, IHR.
1841. var. Bod, IHR.
1847. var. BCL, BLN, IHR.
1849*. LAO, IHR.
1851*. BLN, IHR.
1852. var. LAO, Bod, IHR.
1856*. BLN, IHR.
1859. Bod, IHR.
1860*. BCL, IHR. See Boston Grammar School, *The Boston Election of 1860* (1972).
1865. var. Bod, LCL, IHR.
1868. BPL, IHR.

Grantham
1714. LAO [Anc 13/B/2U; 3 Anc 8/4/1].
1796. LCL, IHR.
1818. GrL, LAO, Bod, IHR, NUL.
1820. var. GrL, Bod, GL, IHR, NUL.
1820*. GrL, LAO, Bod, IHR, NUL.
1826. var. GrL, LAO, Bod, GL, NUL.
1830. var. GrL, LAO, Bod, GL, IHR, NUL.
1831. var. GrL, LAO, Bod, IHR, NUL.
1837. GrL, Bod, NUL.
1852. var. GCL, GrL, Bod, IHR, NUL.
1857. GrL, IHR, NUL.
1865. GrL, Bod, IHR, NUL.
1868. GrL, IHR, NUL.

Lincolnshire continued

Great Grimsby
1818. GyL, LCL, BL, IHR.
1820. GyL, IHR.
1826. GyL, BL, IHR.
1830. var. GyL, HCL, IHR.
1831. GyL, IHR.
1831*. var. GyL, HCL, IHR.
1832. var. GyL, IHR.
1835. GyL.
1852. var. GyL, Bod, IHR.
1862*. GyL, BL, Bod, IHR.
1865, 1868. GyL, BL, IHR.

Horncastle
1836. Church ratepayers. LCL.

Lincoln
1722. LAO [Mon 22/C/26].
1727. LAO [Mon 22/C/24]; Leeds District Archives [Ingilby 2955-6].
1754. LCL, IHR.
1761. LAO, LCL, IHR, NUL.
1768. LCL, GL, IHR, NUL.
1774. LCL, Bod, IHR, NUL.
1780. var. LAO, LCL, Bod, NUL, IHR.
1790. var. LAO, LCL, BL, Bod, GL, NUL, SoG. One of the LCL copies also includes the poll books for **1754, 1761, 1768, 1774** and **1780.**
1806. var. EDL, LAO, LCL, BL, Bod, GL.
1808*. LAO, LCL, BL, Bod, GL.
1818. EDL, LAO, LCL, Bod, IHR, NUL.
1820. LAO, LCL, BL, Bod, IHR, NUL.
1826. var. LAO, LCL, Bod, GL, IHR, NUL. One of the LCL copies also includes the polls for **1806, 1808** and **1818.**
1832. LAO, LCL, BL, IHR, NUL.
1835. var. LAO, LCL, Bod, GL, IHR, NUL.
1837. var. LAO, LCL, Bod, IHR, NUL.
1841. LAO, LCL, GL, NUL.
1847. var. LAO, LCL, Bod, GL, IHR, NUL.
1848*. var. LAO, LCL, EDL, GL, NUL.
1852. var. EDL, LCL, BL, Bod, IHR.
1857. LAO, LCL, BL, Bod, IHR, NUL.
1859. var. LAO, LCL, BL, Bod, IHR, NUL.
1862*, 1865. LAO, LCL, BL, Bod, IHR, NUL.

Stamford
1734. Present location unavailable.
1809*. Bod, IHR, SoG.
1812, 1830, 1831, 1832. Present location unavailable.
1831-32. Burghley House Preservation Trust .
1835 to 1871. Municipal elections: STH [5C/1/1-42].
1837. Elections of Auditors and Assessors: STH [5C/4/1, 5C/3/1].
1847. LCL, BL, CUL: PDL (Wards of St Mary's and All Saints only).
1869. Election of Auditors: STH [5C/4/8].
1873. Election of Assessors: STH [5C/3/23].

LONDON and MIDDLESEX
Abbreviations (national collections, page 14)
CLRO = Corporation of London Records Office.
GL = Guildhall Library.
GLHL = Greater London History Library.
GLRO = Greater London Record Office.
HCL = Hammersmith Central Library (appointment needed with Local History Librarian).
IHR = Institute of Historical Research (see note on page 14).
SoG = Society of Genealogists' Library.

Constituency histories: Seaton (1986), page 12.
Richard Chapman, 'Poll Books for the County of Middlesex', *West Middx. FHS,* **11**.3 (Sep. 1993).

County of Middlesex
1705. var's. Chiswick CL, BL, Bod, GL (copy), IHR; SoG (index to non-resident voters only).
1713 or **1714.** GL; SoG index of voters.
1715. GL, Bod.
1747(?). Warwickshire RO [CR.136/A.253, but date and constituency doubtful].
1750. GLRO [Acc 790/81].
1768. GLRO [MR/PP.1768].
1768. GL, BL.
1768*. GLRO [MR/PP.1768].
1768*. GL, BL.
1769*. GLRO [MR/PP.1769].
1769*. GL, BL; SoG (index to non-resident voters only).
1772, 1784. BL.
1802. var's. GLRO, HCL, Bod, GL, IHR; SoG (also index to non-resident voters).
1806. Tower Division only: GLRO [MR/PP.1806/1].
1820. Tower Division only: GL.

City of London
See W.A. Speck and W.A. Gray, *London Poll Books,* London Record Society **17** (1981).
1682. Election of Lord Mayor: CUL.
1710. GL, IHR, Bod, CUL.
1711. var. Election of Alderman, Broad Street Ward only: GL.
1712. Election of Aldermen, Langbourn Ward only: CLRO.
1713. var. IHR, Bod.
1717, ?1719/20, 1722/3. Election of Common Councilmen: CLRO.
1722. var's. GL (with index), IHR, Bod.
1724*. var. GL, Public Record Office [SP.46/144 f.30], SoG.
1727, 1734. GL.
1768. Bod, GL, IHR.
1771. Election of Bridgemaster: CLRO.
1772. Election of Lord Mayor: CLRO, GL.
1773*. var. GL, IHR, Bod.
1781*. GL.
1784. var. GL, IHR, Bod.
1791, 1807, 1809, 1817, 1818, 1819, 1831(?). Elections of Common Councilmen, Walbrook Ward only: GL.

London and Middlesex: *City of London* continued
1792. SoG, CLRO; GL (Livery lists, checked by the last contested election, in GL only).
1796. var. CLRO, GL, GLHL, IHR.
1823. Election of Aldermen, Langbourn Ward only: CLRO.
1826. Farringdon Without, district 17 only: GL.
1831. Elections for Lord Mayor: GL.
1837. BL.
1861. Election of Lord Mayor: GL.

Additional to the above, the Guildhall Library has a number of MS poll books for minor officials at parish level, including St. Andrew by the Wardrobe (**1764, 1782, 1830, 1838, 1851**), St. Botolph without Aldersgate (**1870, 1872, 1880**), St. Boltolph without Bishopsgate (**1892, 1895**), St. Dionis Backchurch (**1749, 1806, 1875**), St. Helen Bishopsgate (**1835**), St. Katherine Coleman (**1828, 1833**), St. Mary Abchurch with St. Lawrence Pountney (**1736**), St. Mary le Bow (**1778**), St. Peter upon Cornhill (**1828, 1834, 1845, 1877**), St. Stephen Coleman Street (**1697**).

Westminster
Note: GLRO MS holdings are not all in a state fit enough for consultation.
1749. GLRO [WR/PP].
1749*. var. BL, Bod, CUL, GL, GLHL, IHR, SoG. Available on microfiche 013 from SoG. Index at Westminster City Archives.
1774. GLRO [WR/PP].
1774. GL, IHR, SoG.
1780. GLRO [WR/PP].
➤ **1780.** BL, Bod, GL, IHR.
1784. GLRO [WR/PP]; GL.
1788. GLRO [WR/PP]. See Jupp 1973.
1790. GLRO [WR/PP].
1796. GLRO [WR/PP]; GL (part).
1796, 1802. St. Margaret and St. John parishes. Westminster City Libraries Archives Dept.
1802, 1806. GLRO [WR/PP].
1818. var. BL, Bod, GL, GLHL, IHR, Nottingham UL, SoG.
1819, 1820. GLRO [WR/PP].
1832. Paddington only: Archives and Local Studies, Marylebone Library.
1837. Bod, GL, IHR, SoG.
1841. GLRO [WR/PP].
1841. GLHL, Bod, GL, IHR, SoG.

London University
1880. BL.

Monmouthshire - see with **WALES**, page 53.

NORFOLK
Abbreviations (national collections, page 14)
LRO = Lowestoft Branch, Suffolk Record Office.
NCL = Norwich Central Library (including Colman Library).
KCL = King's Lynn Central Library.
MUL = Manchester University Library.
NRO = Norfolk Record Office.
YCL = Great Yarmouth Central Library.

Constituency histories: Seaton (1986), page 12.
R.C. Fiske, 'Changes in parliamentary division and parliamentary representation in Norfolk 1297-1918', *Norfolk Ancestor* **1**.9 (Dec. 1979).

County
1660. GL (poll book?).
1702. Publ. in 'Election for two knights of the shire for Norfolk, 1702: votes polled for Sir Edward Ward, bart.', *Norfolk Record Society* **8** (1936); see also 'A note on the Norfolk election of 1702', *Norfolk Arch.* **37**.3 (1980).
1714/5. NRO.
1714/5. NCL, BL, GL, IHR, SoG.
1734. NRO.
1734. NCL, BL, Bod, GL, IHR, MUL, SoG.
1768. var. KCL, LRO, NCL, BL, Bod, CUL, GL, IHR, MUL, SoG.
1795. MUL.
1795. Election of coroner: GL.
1802. var. KCL, NCL, BL, Bod, GL, IHR, MUL, SoG.
1714, 1734, 1768, 1802. Indexes at SoG, also out-county voters **1710-1830**.
1806. var. KCL, NCL, NRO, BL, Bod, GL, IHR, MUL, SoG. See R.W. Ketton-Cremer, 'The county election of 1806' in *A Norfolk Gallery* (1948).
1817*. var. KCL, LRO, NCL, NRO, BL, Bod, GL, IHR, MUL, SoG. See Jupp, 1973.

East Norfolk
1832. NRO.
1832. LRO, NCL, NRO, BL, Bod, GL, IHR, MUL, SoG.
1832 (Yarmouth only). IHR.
1835. NRO.
1835. KCL, LRO, NCL, NRO, BL, Bod, GL, IHR, MUL, SoG; pub. in *Norfolk Genealogy* **24** (1992).
1837. NRO.
1837. KCL, NCL, NRO, BL, Bod, GL, IHR, MUL, SoG.
1837. NCL (Colman Lib., Yarmouth only).
1839. SoG.
1841. NRO.
1841. LRO, NCL, NRO, Bod, GL, IHR, MUL, SoG.
1858*. var. LRO, NCL, NRO, BL, Bod, GL, IHR, MUL, SoG.
1865. LRO, NCL, NRO, BL, Bod, GL, IHR, SoG.

North Norfolk
1868. NCL, Bod, GL, IHR, SoG.

Norfolk continued

South Norfolk
1868. NCL, BL, Bod, GL, IHR, MUL, SoG.
1871*. NCL, Bod, GL, MUL.

West Norfolk
1835. NRO.
1835. KCL, NCL, BL, Bod, IHR, MUL, SoG.
1837. NRO.
1837. KCL, NCL, BL, Bod, GL, IHR, MUL, SoG.
1839. SoG.
1847. KCL, NCL, BL, GL, MUL, SoG.
1852. NCL, GL, MUL.
1865. KCL, NCL, BL, GL, MUL, SoG.

Great Yarmouth
1754. NCL, Bod, GL, IHR, MUL, SoG.
1777*. NCL, IHR.
1790. NCL, YCL, IHR, SoG.
1795*. NCL, YCL, GL, MUL.
1796. NCL, YCL, Bod, GL, IHR, SoG.
1807. var. NCL, YCL, Bod, GL, IHR, MUL, SoG.
1812. NCL, YCL, GL.
1818. NCL, YCL, GL, IHR, MUL.
1820. NCL, YCL, Bod, GL, IHR, MUL, SoG.
1826. NCL, YCL, Bod, GL, IHR, SoG.
1830. var. KCL, LRO, NCL, YCL, Bod, GL, MUL, SoG.
1831. NCL, YCL, GL, IHR.
1832. var. NCL (Colman Lib.), YCL, GL, IHR, SoG.
1835, 1837, 1838*, 1841, 1847. NCL, YCL, Bod, GL, IHR, SoG.
1848*. var. NCL, YCL, GL, IHR, MUL, SoG.
1852. var. NCL, YCL, Bod, GL, IHR, SoG.
1857. var. NCL, YCL, GL, IHR, MUL.
1859. var. NCL, YCL, GL, IHR, MUL, SoG.
1865. NCL, YCL, GL, IHR, SoG.

King's Lynn (Lynn Regis)
There are four undated eighteenth century poll books in NRO.
1768. KCL, NCL, BL, GL.
1784*. NCL (Colman Lib.), IHR.
1822*. KCL, NCL, BL, Bod, IHR.
1824*, 1826. KCL, NCL, BL, IHR.
1835. NCL (Colman Lib.), BL, IHR.
1852. KCL, NCL, BL, GL.
1865. KCL, NCL (Colman Lib.), GL.
1868. KCL, NCL, IHR.
1869. KCL, IHR.

Norwich
1710. NCL, BL, GL, IHR.
1714/5. var's. NCL, BL, Bod, GL.
1734. NCL, Bod, GL, IHR, MUL, SoG.
1735*. var. NCL, Bod, GL, IHR.
1761. NCL, BL, Bod, GL, IHR, SoG.
1768. var. LRO, NCL, BL, Bod, GL, IHR, MUL, Nat. Lib. Wales, SoG.
1780. NCL, BL, Bod, GL, IHR, SoG.
1781. Election of Sheriff: GL.
1784. NCL, BL, Bod, GL, IHR, SoG.

Norwich continued
1786*. var. NCL, BL, Bod, GL, IHR, SoG.
1787* (with **1786*** added). NCL, BL, GL.
1790. NCL, BL, GL, IHR.
1794*. NCL, BL, GL.
1796. NCL, BL, Bod, GL, IHR, MUL.
1797. Election of Sheriff: GL.
1799*. NCL, BL, GL, IHR, MUL, SoG.
1802. var. NCL, BL, Bod, GL, MUL.
1806. var. NCL, BL, Bod, GL, IHR, MUL, SoG.
1807, 1812, 1818. NCL, BL, Bod, GL, IHR, MUL, SoG.
1830. NCL, LRO, BL, Bod, GL, IHR, MUL.
1832. NCL, BL, Bod, IHR, SoG.
1835. NCL, BL, Bod, IHR, MUL.
1835 (municipal council). BL.
1847. var. NCL, GL, IHR.
1852. NCL, IHR.
1854*. NCL, BL, GL.
1857. var. NCL, GL, IHR, MUL, SoG.
1859. NCL, GL, IHR.
1860*. NCL, BL, IHR.
1865. NCL, IHR, SoG.
1868. NCL, BL, GL, IHR, SoG.
1870*. NCL, BL, Bod, GL, IHR, SoG.
1871*. NCL, GL, SoG.

NORTHAMPTONSHIRE
Soke of Peterborough now in Cambridgeshire.

Abbreviations (national collections, page 14)
MUL = Manchester University Library.
NCoL = Northamptonshire County Library.
NCL = Northampton Central Library.
NLW = National Library of Wales, Aberystwyth.
NRO = Northamptonshire Record Office.
NUL = Nottingham University Library.
PDL = Peterborough Divisional Library.
PMS = Peterborough Museum Society Library.

Constituency histories: Seaton (1986), page 12.

County
(1604). See J.K. Gruenfelder, 'Two Midland parliamentary elections of 1604: Northamptonshire and Worcestershire', *Midland History* **3** (1975).
1695. NRO [C(A)7513/1-2]; NCL.
1702, 1705. NCL, NRO, PDL, PMS, IHR; SoG (also index to non-resident voters). See J. Alsop, 'The Northamptonshire Commission of the Peace **(1702)** and parliamentary polls **(1702, 1705)**', *Northamptonshire Past & Present*. **6**.5 (1981-2); and D.R. Hainsworth and Cherry Walker, *The Correspondence of Lord Fitzwilliam of Milton and Francis Guybon his Steward 1697-1709*, Northamptonshire Record Society **36** (1990).
1730. Nassaburgh Hundred only: GL.
1730*. NCL, NRO, PDL, PMS, BL, Birmingham CL, Bod, GL, MUL, SoG.
1748*. NCL, NRO, PDL, PMS, BL, Bod, GL, IHR, SoG.
1806. NCL, NRO, PDL, PMS, BL, Bod, GL, IHR; SoG (also index to non-resident voters).
1831. var. NCL, NRO, PMS, BL, Bod, CUL, GL, SoG, IHR, MUL, NUL (the last four at least include reprints, though not exact, of 1702, 1705, 1730, 1748 and 1806)
1832. Canvass list, Towcester out-voters only: NCL.

North Northamptonshire
1832. var. NCL, NCoL, BL, Bod, GL, IHR, SoG.
1835*. NCL, NCoL, GL, IHR.
1837. NCL, NCoL, Bod, GL.
1857. BL, GL.

South Northamptonshire
1841. NCL, GL.
1847. NCL, Bod, GL, IHR.
1857. NCL, Bod, GL, IHR, SoG.
1858*. NCL, GL.
1865. NRO, IHR.
1868. var. NRO, NCoL, Bod, GL, NUL.

Brackley
1701, 1702, 1705, 1713, 1734, 1754 (and possibly other years): NRO [Ellesmere (Brackley) Colln. 171/1-33; 1710, also quoted by Speck, below, is not in this collection].
1701, 1702, 1705, 1710, 1713. Printed as appendix to W.A. Speck, 'Brackley: a study in the growth of oligarchy', *Midland History* **3** (1975-6).

Higham Ferrers
c.1640. NRO.

Northampton
172-. GL.
1727. NCL, IHR.
(1734). See D. Paton, 'The Northampton election of 1734: national politics and the local community', *Northants. Past & Present* **7**.3 (1985-6).
1768. var's. NCL, BL, Bod, GL, IHR.
1774. NCL, NRO, BL, GL, IHR.
1784. NCL, NRO, Bod, GL, IHR, MUL.
1790. NCL, NRO, Bod, GL, IHR, MUL, SoG.
1796. NCL, NRO, BL, Bod, IHR.
1818. NCL, NRO, BL, GL, IHR, MUL, SoG.
1820. var. NCL, NRO, BL, Bod, GL, IHR, MUL, NUL, SoG.
1826. var's. NCL, NRO, IHR, BL, Bod, GL, NUL, SoG.
1830. var. NCL, BL, Bod, GL, IHR, MUL, SoG.
1831. var. NCL, Bod, GL, IHR, NUL, SoG.
1832. NCL, Bod, GL, IHR, MUL, SoG.
1835. var. NCL, Bod, GL, IHR, MUL.
1837. var's. NCL, Bod, GL, IHR, MUL.
1841. NCL, IHR, NUL.
1842 (municipal election). NCL.
1852. NRO, NCL, IHR.
1857. NCL, IHR.
1859, 1865. NCL, IHR.

Peterborough
(1700/1). See Hainsworth and Walker, Northamptonshire Record Society **36** (1990) (left).
1727. NRO [Fitzwilliam Misc. Vol. 309].
1835. NCL, NRO, IHR.
1837. var. NRO, NCL, PMS, Bod, IHR.
1841. NRO, Bod, IHR.
1852. NCL, NRO, PMS, IHR; Bod(?).
1852*. var. Bod, NCL, NRO, PMS, IHR.
1853*. NRO, PMS, Bod, IHR, NLW.
1857. NRO, PMS, Bod, IHR.
1859. NCL, NRO, PMS, Bod, IHR.
1865. var. NRO, PMS, IHR.
1868. NCL, PDL, PMS, IHR.
n.d. NLW [Harpton Court 2215].

NORTHUMBERLAND

Abbreviations (national collections, page 14)
BTL = Berwick upon Tweed Library.
BTRO = Berwick upon Tweed Branch, Northumberland Record Office.
DPD = Dept. of Palaeography & Diplomatic, University of Durham.
MCL = County Central Library, Morpeth.
MUL = Manchester University Library.
NCL = Newcastle upon Tyne Central Library.
NRO = Northumberland Record Office, North Gosforth, Newcastle..
NUL = Newcastle upon Tyne University Library.
TWAS = Tyne & Wear Archives Service, Newcastle.

Constituency histories: Seaton (1986), page 12.

County
1698. NRO [NRO.650/C/30; IDE.7/119].
1705. NRO [IDE.7/120-1]; NCL.
1710. NCL, NRO, Bod, GL, SoG. See also **1721/2**, **1734**.
1715/6. NCL, NRO, BL, SoG, MCL. Reprinted in 1899.
1721/2. NCL, NRO, BL, SoG. Reprinted 1898, incl. **1710, 1715/6**, with **North Northumberland 1841**, see below; see also **1734**.
1723*. NCL, GL.
1734. NCL, NRO, NUL, Bod, GL, IHR, SoG; MUL (reprint, incl. **1710, 1721**).
1747/8*. NCL, NRO, NUL, BL, Bod, GL, IHR, SoG, TWAS. Reprinted in 1826.
1774. var. DPD, NCL, NRO, BL, Bod, CUL, TWAS, MUL, SoG. Reprinted in 1826.
1826*. MCL, NCL, Bod, GL, IHR, TWAS, SoG. Reprinted later 1826.
1826. BTL, NRO, IHR, MCL, South Shields CL, TWAS, BL, Bod, GL, SoG. Lists also voters in **1747/8, 1774** and **March 1826**.

North Northumberland
1841. BTL, DPD, MCL, NCL, NRO, BL, Bod, GL, IHR, MUL, SoG. Includes *County* polls for **1722** and (part) **1734**.
1847. NCL, BL, Bod, GL, IHR, MUL, SoG.
1852. BTL, MCL, NRO, BL, Bod, GL, IHR, MUL, SoG.

South Northumberland
1832. MCL, NCL, NRO, Bod, GL, IHR, TWAS, MUL, SoG.
1852. var. NCL, NRO, BL, Bod, GL, IHR, TWAS, MUL, SoG.

Berwick-upon-Tweed
1784, 1802, 1803, 1806, 1812, 1818, 1820 March, 1820 Dec.* BTRO [G.5/1-7].
1820 Dec.*. BL.
1826, 1827*, 1830, 1831, 1832, 1835. BTRO [G.5/8-15].
1847, 1852, BLN, IHR.
1857. National Library of Scotland.
1859, 1859*, 1863*, 1865, 1868. BLN, IHR.

Morpeth
n.d. NRO [IDE.7/122].
1727, 1761. NRO [ZAN.M.16/B9/136,138].
1780, 1784. Canvasser's lists: DPD [H.N. N.57/22, 87/45].
1802. NRO [ZAN.M.16/153].

Newcastle-upon-Tyne
1714/5. Leeds District Archives [BW/P.10].
1722. NCL, IHR.
1723. NRO [ZAN.M.13/A.7].
1734. NCL, BL, Bod, IHR.
1741. var. NCL, NRO, BL, Bod, CUL, GL, IHR, TWAS, MUL, SoG.
1768-1793. Common Council electors' lists: TWAS.
1774. var. NCL, NRO, BL, Bod, GL, IHR, Manchester CL, MUL, TWAS, SoG. See T.R. Knox, 'Wilkism and the Newcastle election of 1774', *Durham University Journal* **72** (1979).
1777*. DPD, NCL, NRO, BL, Bod, GL, IHR, TWAS, MUL, SoG. See T.R. Knox, '"Bowes and liberty": the Newcastle by-election of 1777', *D.U.J.* **77** (1985).
1780. DPD, NCL, NRO, BL, Bod, GL, IHR, TWAS, MUL, SoG.
1820. NCL, NRO, BL, Bod, GL, IHR.
1832. NCL, BL, Bod, GL, IHR, TWAS.
1835. NCL, NRO, BL, Bod, GL, IHR, TWAS, MUL.
1836*. NCL, BL, GL, TWAS, SoG.
1837. NCL, BL, IHR, TWAS.
1847, 1852. NCL, BL, IHR.
1857. Election of Coroner: GL.
1859. NCL, Bod, GL.
1859*. NCL, GL.
1860*. TWAS, IHR, Newcastle Soc. of Antiquaries.

Tynemouth
1837. Present location unavailable.
1852. GL, Tynemouth CL.
1861. BLN, IHR.

NOTTINGHAMSHIRE

Abbreviations (national collections, page 14)
NAO = Nottinghamshire Archives Office.
NCL = Nottingham Central Library.
NkCL = Newark Central Library.
NUML = Manuscripts Dept., University of Nottingham.
NUL = Nottingham University Library.
TSL = Library of the Thoroton Society.

Constituency histories: Seaton (1986), page 12.

County
1698. NAO (TS index in NCL).
1710. Published in *Poll Books of Nottingham and Nottinghamshire 1710*, Thoroton Soc. Record Series **18** (1958). This includes a very detailed biographical index compiled by Violet W. Walker.
1722. NAO, NCL, NUML, IHR, SoG.
1774. NAO (this may be for **Newark** only).

North Nottinghamshire
1832. var. NCL, NUL, IHR, SoG.
1872*. NCL, GL, IHR.

South Nottinghamshire
1846*. NCL, NUL, Bod, GL, IHR, SoG. See J.R. Fisher, 'Issues and influence: two by-elections in south Nottinghamshire in the mid-nineteenth century', *Historical Journal* **24** (1981).
1851*. NCL, IHR, SoG.

East Retford
1802. NUML, IHR.
1831. var. NCL, IHR.

Newark
1765/6. NUML [Ne C 4497; see also 4496 and 4498].
1774. NAO (possibly for **County**).
1780. NkCL, IHR.
1790. NAO, NCL, NkCL, GL.
1796. NAO, NkCL, GL, IHR.
1826. var. NAO, NCL, NkCL, NUL, BL, Bod, GL, IHR.
1829*. var. NAO, NCL, NkCL, NUL, BL, Bod, GL, IHR.
1830. var. NAO, NCL, NkCL, NUL, BL, Bod, GL, IHR; NCL vol. is composite for 1790, 1826 and 1829 also.
1831. BL, IHR, Leicester UL.
1832. NkCL, BL, IHR.
1840*. var. NCL, BL, Bod, IHR, SoG.
1841. NCL, NkCL, BL, IHR.
1847. NAO, NkCL, BL, Bod, IHR.
1852. NAO, NkCL, IHR.
1859. NCL, NkCL, IHR.
1868, 1870*. NkCL, IHR.

Nottingham
See S.N. Mastoris, *Nottingham poll books: a Nottingham finding list* (1980).
1710. NAO [M.686].
1710. Publ. in *Thoroton S.R.S.* **18** (1958) (see left).
1713. NAO [M.688].
1722. NAO.
1747. Election of Common Councilman: NCL.
1754. NAO [M.366, 466].
1754. var. NAO, NCL, NUL, TSL, IHR, SoG. Available as Microfiche 006 from SoG.
1774. NAO [CA.1537].
1774. NAO, NCL, NUL, TSL, BL, GL, IHR.
1780. var. (includes Council's election): NCL, Bod, IHR.
1796. NCL, IHR.
1798. NAO.
1798. Election of Councillors: NCL.
1802. var. NCL, IHR.
1803*. NAO [CA.1538].
1803*. var's. NAO, NCL, NUL, TSL, Bod, IHR.
1806. NAO [CA.1541].
1806. var. NAO, NCL, BL, GL, IHR, SoG.
1807, 1812. NAO [CA.1539, 1540].
1812. NAO, NCL, IHR.
1815. Election of Junior Councilman: NCL.
1818. var's. NCL, NUL, BL, GL, IHR, SoG.
1819. Election of Senior Councilman: NCL.
1820. var. NAO, NCL, NUL, TSL, BL, Bod, GL, IHR.
1825. Election of Senior Councilmen: NAO, NCL, GL.
1826. var. NAO, NCL, NUL, TSL, BL, GL, IHR.
1828. Election of County Coroner: NUL.
1830. var. NAO, NCL, NUL, BL, GL, IHR.
1830. Election of Senior Councilman: NCL.
1832. NAO, NUL, GL, IHR.
1835. Election of Junior Councilman: NAO [CA.1512], includes part of 1832 poll.
1835, 1836. Elections of Junior Councilmen: NAO(?), NCL, NUL.
1841*. NAO, NCL, NUL, Bod, IHR.
1842*. NCL, BLN, IHR.
1843*. NCL, IHR.
1847. NCL, IHR.
1852. NCL, GL, IHR.
1857. BLN, NCL, IHR.
1859, 1861*. BLN. IHR.
1865. var. NCL, IHR, BLN.
1866*. BLN, NCL, NUL, IHR.
1868. NCL, NUL, TSL, IHR.
1869*. NCL,, GL, IHR.

OXFORDSHIRE

Abbreviations (national collections, page 14)
BCL = Banbury Central Library.
Bod = Bodleian Library, Oxford (see note on page 14).
MUL = Manchester University Library.
NUL = Nottingham University Library.
OA = Oxfordshire Archives (formerly Oxfordshire Record Office).
OCA = Oxford City Archives (c/o OCL).
OCL = Oxford Central Library (Centre for Oxfordshire Studies).

Constituency histories: Seaton (1986), page 12.

County

1754. var. OCL, OA, Bod, BL, GL, IHR; SoG (also index to non-resident voters). Banbury and Bloxham Hundreds facsimile reprint (with canvass lists) in J.S.W. Gibson, *The 1754 Election in North Oxfordshire*, offprint from *Cake & Cockhorse* (Banbury Historical Society), **11**.8 (Spring 1991). See E.H. Cordeaux and D.H. Merry, *A Bibliography of Printed Works Relating to Oxfordshire*, Oxford Hist. Soc. **N.S. 11** (1955) and Supplement, O.H.S. **N.S. 28** (1981) for the many contemporary pamphlets relating to this election.
1826. Bod, OCL, OA, GL, IHR, SoG.
1830. Bod, OA, GL, SoG.
1831. Bod, OCL, OA, IHR.
1837. Bod, OCL, OA, BL, IHR, SoG.
1862*. Bod, OA, GL.
c.1865. Canvass book(?): OA (Kidlington only) [CH.CVIII/i/1].

Banbury

(1660-1698). See J.S.W. Gibson, 'The Background to the Surrender of Banbury's Charter in 1683; and the Parliamentary Representation of the Borough, 1660-1698', *Cake & Cockhorse* (Banbury Historical Society), **11**.7 (Autumn 1990).
(1681, 1689/90, 1691, 1700/1, 1705). See J.S.W. Gibson and E.R.C. Brinkworth (eds.), *Banbury Corporation Records: Tudor and Stuart*, Banbury Hist. Soc. **15** (1977).
(1715). See B.S. Trinder and J.S.W. Gibson, 'General Election: 1715-style', *C & CH* (B.H.S.) 3.4 (Summer 1966).
1759, 1766, 1767, 1768, 1774, 1778, 1780, 1783, 1784, 1790, 1792, 1794, 1796, 1802, 1806, 1808, 1812, 1818, 1819, 1820, 1826, 1830, 1831. OA [BB. XIX/3]. See also Bodleian, Dept. of MSS, for correspondence in North MSS utilised by Alan Valentine, *Lord North*, 2 vols. (1967).
(1806-1831). See David Eastwood, 'Politics and Elections in Banbury 1806-1831', *C&CH* (B.H.S.), **11**.9 (Summer 1991). Includes polls for **1806**, **1808** and **1831**.
1835. Bod, IHR.
1837, 1841. Bod, OA, IHR.
1847. var. Bod, OA, IHR.

Banbury continued

(1832-59). See B.S. Trinder, *A Victorian M.P. and his Constituents: The correspondence of H.W. Tancred, 1841-1859*, B.H.S. **8** (1967); and for illustrations of Banbury election posters (only, no related text), Michael Drake, *Introduction to Historical Psephology*, Open University (1974).
1859*. var. BCL, IHR, SoG. Reprinted by the Open University *(D.301. Social Sciences, third level course: Historical data and social sciences, 1974)*, and therefore available in many other libraries.
1859 (with 1865 electoral register), **1865.** BCL, IHR, SoG. Reprint as **1859***.
1868. BL.

Oxford

1768. Bod, OCL, GL.
1790*, 1796*. Bod, OCL, IHR.
1802. Bod, OCL, IHR, SoG.
1806. Bod, OCL, IHR.
1812, 1818, 1820. Bod, OCL, IHR.
1825. Election of Town Clerk: OCL, GL.
1826. Bod, OCL, IHR.
1830. Bod, OCL, IHR.
1832. Bod, OCL.
1835, 1837. Bod, OCL, IHR.
1841. OCA.
1841. var. Bod, OCL, IHR.
1868. Bod, OCA, OCL, IHR.

Oxford University

1722. Bod, BL, IHR.
1737*. Bod, IHR.
1750*. Bod, BL, CUL, GL, IHR.
1768. Bod, BL, CUL, GL, IHR, MUL.
1806. Bod, GL, IHR.
1821*. Bod, BL, GL, SoG.
1829*. Bod, BL, CUL, GL, IHR, MUL, SoG.
1847. Bod, BL, GL, IHR, MUL, NUL.
1852. Bod, BL, CUL, GL, IHR, NUL, SoG.
1853*. var's. Bod, BL, CUL, GL, IHR, MUL, NUL, SoG.
1859. Bod, BL, GL, IHR.
1865. var. Bod, Hampshire RO, BL, GL, SoG.
1878. Bod, BL, CUL, GL, IHR, MUL.

RUTLAND

Abbreviations (national collections, page 14)
LCL = Leicester Central Library.
LRO = Leicestershire Record Office.

Constituency histories: Seaton (1986), page 12.

County
1710. LCL, LRO, Bod, IHR.
1713. LRO [DG.7 Rut 2(iv)].
1722. LCL, LRO, Northamptonshire RO.
1734. SoG (index to non-resident voters only).
1754. Present location unavailable.
1761. LRO, GL; SoG (index to non-resident voters only).
1841. LCL, Bod, CUL, GL.

SHROPSHIRE

Abbreviations (national collections, page 14)
MUL = Manchester University Library.
NLW = National Library of Wales, Aberystwyth.
OTCA = Oswestry Town Council Archives.
SCL = Shrewsbury Central Library.
SS = Shrewsbury School.
SRO = Shropshire Record Office.
UCC = Salisbury Library, University College, Cardiff.

Constituency histories: Seaton (1986), page 12.

County
1676 *[sic].* SCL.
1701, 1702, 1710. NLW [Aston Hall 4402-5].
1713-4. SRO.
1713. SCL, SRO, BL, GL.
1722. SCL, IHR.
1747. SRO.
1768, 1796, 1805, 1806 (canvass books). SRO.
1820. Canvass book: SCL (Wenlock county voters only).
1831. SCL, SRO, BL, GL, Manchester CL, NLW.
1832. SRO.

North Shropshire
1832. SCL, SRO, GL, NLW.
1868. SCL, SRO, Bod, GL.

South Shropshire
1865. var. SCL, SRO, Bod, GL, IHR.
1868. var. SCL, SRO, Bod, GL.

Bishop's Castle
1754, 1763. SRO.
1763-90 *[sic].* SRO.
1818-19, 1819, 1820. SRO.

Bridgnorth
1705, 1741, 1784, 1826, 1830. SRO.
1837. SCL, IHR.
1847. SRO, SS, IHR.
1865. SRO, Bod, IHR.
1868. SRO, IHR.

Shropshire continued

Ludlow
1734, 1741, 1743, 1768, 1770, 1774, 1783, 1784, 1790, 1796, 1802, 1806. SRO.
1832, 1835, 1837. SCL, IHR.
1839. BL.
1840*. SCL, IHR.
1865. SoG.
1868. SCL, IHR.

Oswestry
1850-72. Assessor elections: OTCA [E.8].
1852-65. Council elections: OTCA [E.7].

Shrewsbury
1708. SRO.
1734. SCL, SRO, IHR, NLW.
1747. NLW [NLW MS 7988C].
1747. SCL, GL; published in *Shropshire Arch. Soc. Transactions*, **1st series, 3** (1880).
1768. SCL.
1768. var. SRO.
1774. SCL.
1774. Public Record Office [C.109/72].
1796. SCL, SRO, BL, Bod, GL, IHR, NLW, UCC. See A.P. Jenkins, 'Two Shropshire elections of the late eighteenth [Shrewsbury 1796] and early nineteenth centuries [North Shropshire 1876]', *Caradoc & Severn Valley Field Club Trans.* **16** (1968).
1806. var. SCL, SRO, Bod, IHR, MUL.
1807. var. SCL, SRO, Bod, IHR, MUL, NLW.
1812. var. SCL, SRO, Bod, IHR, MUL, NLW, UCC.
1814*. SCL, SRO, Bod, IHR.
1819*. var. SCL, SRO, Bod, IHR.
1822. Canvasser's list: SRO.
1826. var. SCL, SRO, Bod, IHR.
1830. SCL, SRO, Bod, IHR, NLW.
1831. SCL, SRO, Bod, IHR.
1832. SCL, SRO, Bod, IHR, MUL, NLW.
1835. SCL (municipal as well as parliamentary); SRO, Bod, IHR, MUL, NLW.
1835. Poll book of Burgesses: GL, Manchester CL.
1837. var. SCL, SRO, Bod, IHR, MUL.
1838. Municipal only: SCL.
1841. SCL, SRO, Bod, IHR, NLW.
1847. var. SCL, SRO, Bod, GL, IHR, NLW.
1848-9. NLW (Castle Ward only) [NLW MS 7988.C].
1852. SCL, SRO, Bod, IHR, NLW.
1855. NLW (Castle Ward only) [NLW MS 7988.C].
1857. var. SS, SRO, Bod, IHR, MUL, NLW.
1862*. var's. SCL, SRO, SS, IHR, Manchester CL, NLW.
1868. SCL, SRO, Bod, IHR.
1870*. SCL, SRO, IHR.

Wenlock
1820. See under **County**, left.
1832, 1835. SRO, GL.

SOMERSET

Abbreviations (national collections, page 14)
BaCL = Bath Central Library
BCL = Bristol Central Library.
BgCL = Bridgwater Central Library.
BMB = Blake Museum, Bridgwater.
BRO = Bath Record Office.
SRO = Somerset Record Office, Taunton.
TLH = Taunton Local History Library.

Constituency histories: Seaton (1986), page 12.

County
1714. SRO [Q/REp + DD/WY 6x 36].
1807, 1818, 1826, 1832. SRO [Q/REp].

East Somerset
1832. BaCL, IHR.

West Somerset
1835, 1837. SRO [Q/REp].

Bath
1832. var. BaCL, BCL, BRO, BL, IHR.
1835. BaCL, BCL, GL.
1837. var. BaCL, BCL, BL, GL, Bod, IHR; SoG (last includes polls of **1832, 1835** by same voters).
1841. var. BaCL, BCL, GL, IHR, SoG. One variant includes polls for 1832, 1835 and 1837.
1847. var. BaCL, BCL, BRO, BL, Bod, IHR, SoG. One variant includes poll for 1841.
1851*. BaCL, BCL, BRO, IHR.
1852. BaCL, BCL, BRO, BL, IHR.
1855*. BaCL, BCL, BRO, BL, IHR, SoG. Reprinted by Open University (1974).
1857. BaCL, BCL, BRO, BL, IHR, SoG.
1859. var. BaCL, BCL, IHR, SoG.
1868. BaCL, BCL, IHR.
(1832-68). See Michael Drake, 'Radical Bath', in *Introduction to Historical Psephology* (Open University, 1974).

Bridgwater
1754, 1806, 1807. BMB, BgCL, SRO, IHR.
1780, 1790, 1802. BgCL, IHR.
1818. var. BMB, BgCL, SRO, IHR.
1826. BMB, BgCL, SRO, IHR.
1831. var. BMB, BgCL, SRO, IHR.
1835. BMB, BgCL, SRO, IHR.
1837*, 1841. SRO [D/B/bW 38/3].
1837*, 1841. BMB, BgCL, SRO, IHR.
1847. var. BMB, BgCL, SRO, IHR.
1852. var. BMB, BgCL, SRO, IHR.
1857. BMB, BgCL, SRO, IHR.
1865. var. BMB, BgCL, SRO, IHR.
1866 June*, July*. BMB, BgCL, SRO, IHR.

Minehead
1747. SRO [DD/WY bx 36].

Taunton
1695, 1698. SRO [DD/SF 1090, 1094].
1700. SRO [DD/SAS TN.159/2].
1710. SRO [DD/SAS TN.40 + DD/SAS TN.159/3].

Taunton continued
1774. SRO, IHR.
1818. TLH, IHR.
1832, 1834. Manuscript votes cast: TLH, IHR.
(1835*). See R.E. Foster, 'Peel, Disraeli and the 1835 Taunton by-election', *Somerset Arch. & Nat. Hist. Soc. Proceedings* **126** (1982).
1837. SRO, IHR.
1853*. BLN, IHR.

Wells
1765. BL.

STAFFORDSHIRE

Abbreviations (national collections, page 14)
BHL = Brierley Hill District Library, local collection.
BRL = Birmingham Reference Library, Local Studies Dept. (printed) and Archives Dept. (MSS).
JRO = Lichfield Joint Record Office.
LL = Lichfield Library.
NL = Newcastle under Lyme Library.
SL = Stafford Library.
SRO = Staffordshire Record Office.
STL = Stoke on Trent Central Library.
TCL = Tamworth Central Library.
WLHC = Walsall Local History Centre.
WSL = William Salt Library.

Constituency histories: Seaton (1986), page 12.

County
1740. Suit roll indicating voting interest: NL (MF).
1747. WSL, BRL, SL, GL, IHR; NL (MF).
1747 (Totmonslow Hundred only) Hereford RO, IHR.

North Staffordshire
1832. WSL, BRL, GL, IHR, SoG.
1837. WSL, GL.
1865. STL, BRL, GL.

South Staffordshire
1835*. SL, WLHC, WSL, IHR.
1835. BHL (Seisdon Hundred only).
(1841). See P.J. Doyle, 'The general election of 1841: the representation of South Staffordshire', *South Staffs. Arch. & Hist. Soc. Trans.* **12** (1970/1).

West Staffordshire
1868. BHL, LL, SL, WLHC, WSL, BRL, CUL, GL, Wolverhampton CL, SoG.

Lichfield
1710, 1714, 1718, 1721, 1727. BRL [379746-50]; LL.
1747. SRO, IHR.
1755. BRL [379751]; LL.
1761. LL.
1799*. BRL [379753]; JRO [D.15/4/4/1-4].
1799*. var. LL, SRO, WSL, IHR.
1826. JRO [D.15/4/5/2-5, -4 incl. sums of money against names].

Staffordshire: Lichfield continued
1830, 1831. JRO [D.15/4/9/5; D.15/4/7/1].
1831. Canvass books, notes: JRO [D.15/4/7/2-3].
1832, 1835. JRO [D.15/4/8/1; D.15/4/9/4-5].
1835. LL, IHR.
1837. Canvass list: JRO [D.15/4/10/3].
1841(?). Canvass notes: JRO [D.15/4/11/4-7].
1843, 1848. Polls for assistant overseer of the poor, St. Chad's parish only: JRO [D.15/4/11/9].

Newcastle-under-Lyme
1675. NL (MF).
1724. NL.
1734. NL, IHR.
1752. Suit roll showing voting interest: NL.
1774. NL, IHR.
1790. IHR.
1792*. NL, IHR.
1793*. SRO, IHR; NL (MF).
1802. NL, SRO, IHR.
1807. NL, IHR.
1812. var. NL, GL, WSL, IHR.
1815*. NL, WSL, IHR.
1818. NL, SRO, IHR.
1820. NL, IHR.
1823*. NL, WSL, IHR.
1830. NL, WSL, IHR.
1831. var. NL, WSL, IHR.
1832. var. NL, WSL, GL, IHR.
1835. WSL, IHR.
1837. NL, GL.
1841. GL.
1841. NL, WSL, IHR.
1842. NL (copy).
1857. Present location unavailable.
1865. NL, IHR.

Stafford
1780. WSL, GL.
1790, 1807. WSL, IHR.
1812. WSL, BL, IHR.
1818. WSL, GL.
1826, 1830, 1831, 1832, 1835. WSL, IHR.
1837. WSL, GL.
1841, 1847. WSL, IHR.
1852. var. WSL, IHR.
1857. WSL, BL, IHR.
1859, 1860*. WSL, IHR.
1865. WSL, BL, GL.
1868. WSL, IHR.
1869*. var. WSL, IHR; Derby CL (last copy also has 1868 poll).

Stoke on Trent
1832. WSL, IHR.
1837. GL.
1841. STL, IHR.
1847. IHR.
1859, 1862*. STL, IHR.
1865. var. STL, GL, IHR.
1868*. STL, IHR.

Tamworth
1741. BRL [328827].
1761. TCL, Bod, GL.
1818. Present location unavailable.
1837. GL.
1841. WSL, GL.
1868, 1872*. TCL, IHR.

Walsall
1832. WLHC.
1841. WLHC [266/28].
1841. WLHC, Bod.
1847. WLHC [366/30].
1847. WLHC.

SUFFOLK

Abbreviations (national collections, page 14)
BCL = Bury St. Edmunds Central Library.
BRO = Bury St. Edmunds Branch, Suffolk Record Office.
LRO = Lowestoft Branch, Suffolk Record Office.
MUL = Manchester University Library.
NCL = Norwich Central Library.
SRO = Suffolk Record Office, Ipswich.

Constituency histories: Seaton (1986), page 12.

County
1700/1. BRO; SRO (MF).
1702. SRO.
1702. BCL, NCL, IHR; BRO (MF).
1705. SRO, IHR, SoG; BRO (copy).
1710. BCL, BRO, SRO, NCL, BL, Bod, GL, IHR.
1727. BRO, LRO, NCL, SRO, BL, Bod, GL, IHR; SoG (also index to non-resident voters).
(1768). Alsop, J.D. 'Contemporary remarks on the 1768 election in Norfolk and Suffolk', *Norfolk Arch.* **38** (1981).
1784. BRO, NCL, SRO, BL, Bod, IHR, SoG.
1790. BRO, LRO, NCL, SRO, BL, Bod, GL, IHR, MUL; SoG (also index to non-resident voters).
1830. SRO.
1830. NCL, SRO, BL, Bod, GL, IHR, MUL, SoG.

East Suffolk
1832. SRO.
1832. NCL, SRO, Bod, GL, IHR, MUL, SoG.
1835. SRO.
1835. BRO, NCL, SRO, Bod, GL, IHR, SoG.
1839, 1840, *1841.* SRO.
1841. NCL, SRO, BL, GL, SoG.
1843.* SRO.
1843*. LRO, NCL, SRO, BL, IHR.
1859. NCL, SRO, GL, IHR, SoG.
1868. NCL, SRO, GL.

Suffolk continued

West Suffolk
1830, 1832. BRO.
1832. NCL, SRO, BL, Bod, IHR.
1835. BRO.
1835. SRO, Bod.
1837. BRO.
1859. NCL, SRO, GL.
1868. BRO, NCL, SRO. GL, MUL.

Aldeburgh
1812. BRO, SRO, IHR.

Bury St. Edmunds
1754, 1780, 1796, 1807, 1808, 1827. BRO.
1832. var. BRO, NCL, SRO, BL, GL, IHR, SoG.
1835. var. BRO, NCL, SRO, BL, IHR.
1837. BRO, SRO, IHR.
1841. BRO, NCL, SRO, Bod, IHR.
1847. var. BRO, SRO, BLN, IHR.
1852. var. BRO, NCL, GL, BLN, IHR.
1852*. BLN, GL, IHR.
1857. var. BRO, SRO, BLN, IHR.
1859. BLN, IHR.
1865. BLN, BRO, IHR.
1868. BRO, NCL, SRO, IHR.

Ipswich
1741. Bod, GL; NCL, SoG (newspaper reprint 1890).
1741. Supplement (non-voting freemen etc.): IHR, GL.
1754. 'Poll of the bailives': NCL.
1768. BRO, NCL, SRO, Bod, GL, IHR, SoG.
1780. BRO, NCL, SRO, Bod, GL.
1784. NCL, BL, Bod, IHR.
1784*. NCL, Bod, GL, IHR.
1790. NCL, SRO, Bod, GL, IHR.
1806. NCL, SRO, GL, IHR.
1806. Election of Bailiffs and Town Clerk: BL, GL.
1807. var. BRO, NCL, SRO, BL, Bod, GL.
1817. var. Election of Commissioners for Paving and Lighting: GL; Clerk to Commissioners: BL.
1818. var. NCL, SRO, BL, Bod, GL, IHR, SoG.
1818. var. Election of Commissioners for Paving and Lighting: BL.
1820. var. NCL, SRO, BL, Bod, GL, IHR, MUL.
1823. Election of Bailiffs and Town Clerk: BL, GL, SoG.
1823. var. Election of Collectorship of Duties on Coals (also Rates and Assessments): BL.
1825. Election of Bailiffs and Town Clerk: BL.
1826. NCL, SRO, Bod, GL, IHR.
1831. NCL, SRO, Bod, GL, IHR, SoG.
1831. Election of Recorder: BL, GL.
1832. NCL, SRO, BL, Bod, GL, IHR, MUL.
1835. NCL, SRO, BL, Bod, GL, IHR, MUL, SoG.
1835*. NCL, SRO, IHR.
1839*. NCL, SRO, BL, GL, IHR.
1841. NCL, SRO, BL, Bod, GL.
1842 June*. BRO, NCL, Bod, GL, IHR.
1842 Aug.* NCL, SRO, BL, GL, SoG.

Ipswich continued
1847. var. BRO, NCL, SRO, BL, Bod, GL, IHR, MUL, SoG.
1852. var. NCL, SRO, BL, Bod, GL, IHR, SoG.
1857. NCL, SRO, Bod, GL, IHR, SoG.
1859. var. NCL, SRO, BL, Bod, GL, IHR, MUL, SoG.
1865. var. NCL, SRO, Bod, GL, IHR.
1868. NCL, SRO, Bod, GL, IHR, MUL, SoG.

Sudbury
1780. SRO (or BRO?) [Hippesley papers].
1826, 1828*, 1831, 1832 var., 1834*, 1835, 1837, 1837*, 1838*. Present location unavailable.
1837. Facsimile reprint (1990), SoG.
1841. BL.

SURREY

Abbreviations (national collections, page 14)
BL = British Library.
CCL = Croydon Central Library.
GCL = Guildford Central Library.
GL = Guildhall Library, London (see note on page 14).
GMR = Guildford Muniment Room, Surrey Record Office (*Note.* The main Surrey Record Office at Kingston does not hold any poll books, the collection there having been destroyed in the war).
IHR = Institute of Historical Resarch (see note on page 14).
ML = Minet Library (Lambeth Archives Department), 52 Knatchbull Road, London SE5 9QY.

Constituency histories: Seaton (1986), page 12.

County
1705. GCL, BL, Bod, GL, IHR; SoG (index to non-resident voters only).
1710. CCL, GCL, BL, Bod, IHR.
1717. BL [Add. Mss. 11,571].
1719*. ML, IHR.
1727. CCL [fS.60 9324 POL].
1741/2. BL [Add. Mss. 39,291].
1741/2. GL; SoG (index to non-resident voters only); also at SoG, TS. of those voting for Lord Baltimore only, taken from printed copy possibly at IHR.
1774. CCL, GCL, GMR, BL, GL, IHR.
1775*. GCL, GMR, BL, Bod, GL, IHR, SoG. Facsimile reprint with index, West Surrey**1792.** SoG, CLRO; GL (Livery lists, checked by the last contested election, in GL only).
FHS.
1780. GCL, GMR, BL, Bod, GL, IHR, SoG.
1812. GMR (Woking Hundred and Guildford only).
1826. GMR, ML, Bod, IHR.

Surrey continued
East Surrey
1865. GMR, ML, GL, IHR.
West Surrey
1835. GCL, GMR, Bl.
1837. GCL, IHR.
1849*, 1852. GCL, GMR, IHR.
1857. GCL, IHR.
1868. GCL, GL.
Guildford
See R.J. Dabner, 'The Guildford Poll Books', *Root & Branch* (West Surrey F.H.S.) **8**.3 (1981).
1685, 1702 (1713?), ***1708, 1710, 1713/4, 1734, 1761.*** GMR.
1790. GCL, GMR, BL, IHR.
1796, 1806, 1807, 1818, 1830, 1831, 1833, 1835. GMR.
1835. GCL, GMR, IHR.
1837. GMR.
1841. GMR; BL [8135,f.15-16]..
1841. GCL, IHR.
1847, 1852, 1857. GCL, GMR, IHR.
1858*. GCL, GMR, GL.
1865, 1866*, 1868. GCL, GMR, IHR.
Haslemere
1722, 1754. GMR.
1761. GMR, IHR.
Southwark
1747. GL (?).

SUSSEX

Abbreviations (national collections, page 14)
BCL = Brighton Central Library.
CRL = Chichester Reference Library.
ESRO = East Sussex Record Office, Lewes.
HCL = Hastings Central Library.
KAO = Kent Archives Office.
SAS = Sussex Archaeological Society, Barbican House, Lewes.
WDL = Worthing (South Eastern) Divisional Library.
WSRO = West Sussex Record Office, Chichester.

Constituency histories: Seaton (1986), page 12.

County
1705. Publ., '(from a MS. poll book)', in *Miscellaneous Records*, Sussex Record Soc. **4** (1905).
1710. ESRO [DAN 2188-9].
1713. BL, GL (London and Middlesex out voters).

Sussex: *County* continued
1733/4. Canvass lists: KAO [U.269/O 114].
1734. ESRO [ASH 3225]; extracts in *Sussex Arch. Collections* **23** (1871).
1734. BCL, WDL, KAO, ESRO, WSRO, Bod, GL, IHR, SoG. Available as Microfiche 007 from SoG.
1774. BCL, ESRO, WSRO, BL, Bod, GL, IHR, SoG (also index to non-resident voters).
1784. WDL.
1790. SoG (index to non-resident voters only; location of original unknown).
1807. Rape of Bramber only: GL.
1820. var. BCL, CRL, ESRO, WLD, WSRO, Tunbridge Wells Lib., Bod, GL, IHR, Manchester UL, SoG. See S. Excell, 'The Sussex election of 1820', *Sussex FHS Journal* **7**.1 (June 1986).
1820. SoG (Rape of Hastings only)
East Sussex
1832. BCL, ESRO, Bod, GL; SoG (elec. reg. with votes added).
1837. var. BCL, ESRO, WDL, BL, Bod, GL, IHR.
West Sussex
1837. WSRO, GL.
c.1850 (Broadwater parish only). WDL, IHR
Arundel
1741. WSRO [Add. MS 12935].
Brighton
1832. BCL, Bod, GL.
1835. BCL, Bod, GL, SoG.
1837. BCL, WDL, Bod, GL, IHR.
1841. var. BCL, GL, IHR, SoG.
1842*. BCL, WDL, IHR.
1847, 1852. BCL, WDL, GL, Bod, IHR, SoG.
1857. BCL, WDL, GL,IHR, SoG.
1859. BCL, WDL, IHR, SoG.
Chichester
1781. WSRO [Add. MS 2133].
1782. WDL, WSRO, IHR.
1784. WSRO [Add. MS 13391].
1784. BL.
1791, 1793. WSRO.
1823*. GL, WSRO.
1826. SAS, GL, WSRO.
1830. BL, GL, WSRO.
1831. WSRO [Add. MS 2693].
1831. BL, GL.
1837. BL.
Hastings
1722. Bod, IHR.
1832. Hastings Museum, HCL, IHR.
1835, 1847. HCL, IHR.
1865. Present location unavailable.
1868. HCL, GL, IHR, SoG.
Horsham
1770, 1806. SoG (index to non-resident voters only; location of originals unknown).
1847. GL.

Sussex continued

Lewes
1734. WDL, ESRO, Bod, GL, IHR, Manchester UL, SoG.
1768. ESRO, SAS, Bod, IHR.
1774, 1780. ESRO, SAS, IHR.
1790. ESRO, SAS, GL.
1796. ESRO, GL.
1802. ESRO, GL, IHR; pub. on m'fiche (with 1812 and 1826), £2.20, Brooks Davies & Co., Cambria House, 37 Pembroke Avenue, Hove, E. Sussex BN3 5DB.
1809. Election of Coroner: GL.
1812. var. ESRO, IHR, GL; m'fiche as 1802.
1816*. ESRO, GL, SoG.
1818. WDL, ESRO, SAS, IHR.
1826. ESRO, SAS, GL, IHR; m'fiche as 1802.
1830. var. ESRO, SAS, GL, IHR.
1835. var. ESRO, SAS, GL, IHR.
1837*. SAS, GL.
1837. var. ESRO, GL, SoG.
1841. var. ESRO, SAS, GL.
1847, 1859. ESRO, GL.
1865, 1868. WDL, ESRO, GL, IHR, SoG.

Midhurst
1708, 1710, 1711, 1716, 1735/6, 1737/8, 1741, 1744, 1747, 1754. WSRO [for ref. nos. see A.A. Dibben, *The Cowdray Archives*, p.311 ff].

New Shoreham
1784. WSRO, IHR.
1807. GL.
1832. WDL [S.324 COW].
1837. WSRO [Add. MS 1096].

New Shoreham and Bramber
1841. CRL, WDL, SAS, IHR.
1865. WDL, WSRO, IHR.

Rye
1832. BL.
1868. ESRO, SAS, IHR.

Seaford
1761. ESRO [SEA 438]; publ. in S.A.C. 44 (1901); and in S. Excell, 'Voters in Seaford Borough in 1761', *Sussex FH*, **8**.3 (September 1988).
1786, 1794, 1796, 1806, 1807*. ESRO [SEA 458, 467, 474, 478, 480].

WARWICKSHIRE
Abbreviations (national collections, page 14)
BRL = Birmingham Reference Library, Local Studies Dept. (printed) and Archives Dept. (MSS).
CCL = Coventry Central Library.
CvRO = Coventry Record Office.
LSL = Leamington Spa Library.
SBT = Shakespeare Birthplace Trust Record Office, Stratford-upon-Avon.
WL = Warwick Library.
WRO = Warwickshire Record Office, Warwick.

Constituency histories: Seaton (1986), page 12.

County
1705. SBT; WRO (copy?).
1774. BRL, CCL, WRO, BL, Bod, GL, IHR, SoG.
1820*. BRL, LSL, SBT, WL, WRO, Bod, GL, IHR, SoG.
c.1825. Canvass list: BRL (Aston Manor and Birmingham only) [254573-4].

North Warwickshire
1832. BRL, WRO, GL, SoG.
1834. Canvassers' notebook (various parishes). Present location unavailable.
1835. BRL, CCL, GL, SoG.
1837. BRL, CCL, GL.
1868, 1868. BRL (Aston Manor only, street canvass list) [259300, 259200].

South Warwickshire
1832. BRL, WL, IHR.
1836*. BRL, WRO, BL, GL, IHR.
1865. var. BRL, WL, WRO, BLN, LSL, SBT, Bod, GL, IHR, Manchester UL, SoG.
1868. BRL, CCL, WL, WRO, LSL, SBT, GL, IHR, SoG.

Birmingham
1837. BRL, IHR, SoG.
1841. Agent's book for St. Paul's Ward: BRL [260359].
1841. BRL, IHR.
1868. BRL [72002].

Coventry
1741. Bod, IHR.
1747*. BRL, IHR; CCL (copy).
1761. var. BRL, CCL, BL, IHR.
1768*. SBT.
1768*. CCL, IHR.
1774. var. CCL, CvRO, IHR.
1780. CCL, IHR.
1790. BRL, CCL, CvRO, IHR.
1802. CCL, CvRO, IHR.
1803*, 1818, 1820. CCL, IHR.
1826. CCL, IHR.
1833*. CCL, IHR.
1835. CCL, GL.
1837. var. CCL, IHR.
1841, 1847, 1851*. CCL, IHR.
1857, 1859, 1863*. CCL, CvRO, IHR.

Warwickshire: *Coventry* continued
1865*, 1865. CCL, GL.
1867*. CCL, CvRO, Bod, IHR.
1868*. 1868. CCL, CvRO, IHR.

Stratford-upon-Avon
1838. Council election: SBT.

Tamworth
1761. WRO (typescript copy).

Warwick
1784. GL.
1792*. Bod, IHR.
1831. var. WRO, BL, Bod, CUL, GL, IHR, SoG.
1832. WRO, IHR.
1835. WRO, University of Warwick (Modern Records Centre) [MSS.21/1330/89], IHR.
1837. WRO, IHR.
1851. Canvass book: BRL [463087].
1852, 1865, 1868. WRO, IHR.

WESTMORLAND
Now part of Cumbria.

Abbreviations (national collections, page 14)
CaL = Carlisle Library.
CaRO = Cumbria Record Office, Carlisle.
KRO = Kendal Branch, Cumbria Record Office.

Constituency histories: Seaton (1986), page 12.

County
(C17-18). See R. Hopkinson, 'The electorate of Cumberland and Westmorland in the late seventeenth and early eighteenth centuries', *Northern History* **15** (1979).
(1741). MS journal of Robert Lowther of Meaburn kept during 1741 election: CaRO [D/Lons/L].
1761, 1768. KRO [WD/Hoth/Box 31].
1768. CaL, Bod, GL, IHR, SoG.
1774. Bod, IHR.
1818. var. CaRO, CaL, Bod, GL, IHR, SoG.
1820. var. Barrow CL, CaL, CaRO (separate polls for all four Wards) [D/Lons/L], KRO, IHR, BL, Bod, GL, SoG.
1826. var. CaL, KRO, GL, IHR, SoG; CaRO (except Kendal Ward) [D/Lons/L].
1832. CaRO (separate polls for all four Wards); KRO, GL.
1837, 1842, 1854, 1865. CaRO [D/Lons/L].

Appleby
1700, 1701, 1702, 1708, 1710, 1713, 1723. KRO [WD/Hoth/Box 38].
1754. KRO [WD/Hoth/Boxes 36-7]; CaRO [D/Lons/Appleby 1754].
1796, 1807. KRO [WD/Hoth/Box 39, 38].

WILTSHIRE
Abbreviations (national collections, page 14)
DM = Devizes Museum.
WAS = Wiltshire Archaeological and Natural History Society, Devizes Museum.
WRO= Wiltshire Record Office, Trowbridge.

Constituency histories: Seaton (1986), page 12.

County
1705. DM.
1705. GL, IHR, SoG.
1772*. WRO [A.1/340/1], DM.
1772*. WRO, BL, Bod, GL, IHR, Manchester UL, SoG. Available as Microfiche 008 from SoG.
1818. WRO [A.1/340/3].
1818. DM, BL, Bod, GL, IHR, Manchester UL, SoG.
1819. WRO [A.1/340/4].
1819*. DM, BL, GL, IHR.
1833, 1837. WRO [A.1/340/5,6].

South Wiltshire
1865. DM, GL.

Chippenham
1841, 1865, 1868. WAS, IHR.

Cricklade
1784. Swindon CL, GL, SoG.
1831. Swindon CL, IHR.
1837. GL (with register of voters and canvass).
1859. WAS, IHR.
1865. BLN, IHR.
1868. WAS, GL, IHR.

Devizes
1844*, 1857, 1859, 1863*. BLN, IHR.
1868. var. BLN, IHR.

Malmesbury
1868. Bod.

Salisbury
1765*. BLN, HR.
1833. Present location unavailable.
1836. Local election. Present location unavailable.
1843*, 1853*, 1865, 1868. BLN, IHR.

Wootton Bassett
1790. WRO [A.1/340/2].

WORCESTERSHIRE
Now part of Hereford & Worcester.

Abbreviations (national collections page 14)
BRL = Birmingham Reference Library, Local Studies Dept. (printed) and Archives Dept. (MSS).
KCL = Kidderminster Central Library.
SHRO = St. Helen's, Hereford & Worcester C.C. Record Office, Worcester.
WRO = HQ, Hereford & Worcester C.C. Record Office, County Hall, Worcester.

Constituency histories: Seaton (1986), page 12.

County
(**1604**). See J.K. Gruenfelder, 'Two Midland parliamentary elections of **1604**: Northamptonshire and Worcestershire', *Midland History* **3** (1975).
c.1705. BRL [505435].
c.1713. SHRO.
1714/5. KCL, SHRO, GL.
1741. BRL, WRO, Bod, IHR, SoG.
1806. GL.
1831, 1835. WRO.

East Worcestershire
1832 (Droitwich, Pershore and Stourbridge Divisions). WRO.

West Worcestershire
1835. IHR, SoG.

Bewdley
1713-19, 1731-61. 'Books of elections': WRO.

Evesham
1780. SoG (early copy, location of original unknown).
1818. SHRO.
1832. Canvass book and list of voters: SHRO.
1841-1880. Canvassers' poll books: SHRO.
1847. Check poll book: SHRO.
1852, 1865. SHRO.
1865. SHRO (Bengeworth only).
1868. Canvass book: SHRO.

Kidderminster
1849*. 1865. KCL, IHR.
1868. Bod [22774 e.107].

Worcester
1741. BRL, IHR.
1747. KCL (copy of poll claimed to be in BRL, Worcester City only, no votes recorded); SoG (index to non-resident voters only).
1747. Bod, GL.
1761. Bod, IHR.
1841. BRL, IHR.
1847, 1852. WRO: Indexes only.
1865. BRL, IHR.
1868. BRL, GL.

YORKSHIRE
Abbreviations (national collections, page 14)
BCL = Beverley Central Library.
BnL = Bridlington Library.
BrCL = Bradford Central Library.
BrDA = Bradford District Archives.
ByCL = Barnsley Central Library.
CAM = Cleveland County Archives Dept., Middlesbrough.
DCL = Dewsbury Central Library.
HAO = Humberside Archive Office, Beverley.
HCL = Hull Central Library.
HdCL = Huddersfield Central Library.
HdM = Huddersfield Museum.
HxCL = Halifax Central Library.
KL = Keighley Library.
LCL = Leeds Central Library.
LDA = Leeds District Archives.
MCL = Manchester Central Library.
MUL = Manchester University Library.
NAO = Nottinghamshire Archives Office.
NUL = Nottingham University Library.
NUML = Manuscripts Dept., University of Nottingham.
NYRO = North Yorkshire Record Office.
RCL = Brian O'Malley Central Library, Rotherham.
ScCL = Scarborough Central Library.
SCL = Sheffield Central Library.
SRO = Sheffield Record Office.
WCL = Wakefield Central Library.
YCL = York Central Library.
YML = York Minster Library.

Constituency histories: Seaton (1986), page 12.

County
(**early C.18**). See J.F. Quinn, 'Yorkshiremen go to the polls: county contests in the early eighteenth century', *Northern History* **21** (1985).
1708. YML [MS Add. 235].
1727. SRO [M/F A 110].
1734 (Canvass book, Agbrigg and Morley Wapentakes only). LDA [TN/PO 10/7, 14].
1734. BrCL, BrDA, Castle Howard Archives, Doncaster Archives Dept., SRO, YML, BL, IHR.
1741. LDA [TN/PO 10/6].
1741 (West Riding only). BrDA [Spencer Stanhope MS 11/5/3/18].
1741 (present area of Kirklees, plus Penistone and Ingbirchworth only). HdCL.
1741/2*. var. BCL, BrCL, DCL, HCL, HdCL, LCL, SCL, SRO, WCL, YCL, YML, BL, Bod, GL, IHR; SoG (also index of non-resident voters). See J. Black, 'Eighteenth century electioneering: a Yorkshire example', Yorks. Arch. J. 59 (1987).
1784. SRO [181/ZI/1]; LDA (canvass books) [RA (acc. 1896)]. See N.C. Phillips, *Yorkshire and English National politics 1783-4* (1961).
1806. SRO. See Jupp 1973.
1807. LDA [HAR (elections) 6]; Chetham's Library, Manchester [MS transcript: MUN D.1.2, Assheton Tonge].

Yorkshire: *County* continued
1807. BCL, BrCL, ByCL, DCL, HAO, HCL, Hull RO, HdCL, LDA, Lincs AO, LCL, RCL, SRO, WCL, YCL, YML, NYRO, BL, Bod, GL, IHR, MUL, SoG.
1830. HAO.

Yorkshire East Riding
1837. BCL, HAO, HCL, Bod, GL, IHR, SoG.
1868. BCL, HAO, HCL, Hull RO, YCL, YML, IHR.

Yorkshire North Riding
1829. Election of Registrar of Deeds: BL.
1868. Canvasser's book for Graisdale, Whitby, only (private ownership).

Yorkshire West Riding
1809. Election of Registrar of Deeds: ByCL, SCL, BL, GL.
1817. Election of Registrar of Deeds: ByCL, GL.
1832. YML.
1835*. var. BrCL, ByCL, DCL, HdCL, LCL, SCL (Sheffield district only), WCL, YCL, YML, BL, Bod, GL, IHR, MUL, SoG.
1836. Election of Registrar of Deeds: BrCL.
1837. BrCL, ByCL, HdCL, KL, LCL, LDA, SCL, WCL, YCL, BL, Birmingham Ref Lib, Bod, GL, IHR, MUL, SoG.
1841. BrCL, ByCL, DCL, KL, LCL, LDA, RCL, SCL, SRO, WCL, YML, MCL, Bod, GL, IHR, MUL, SoG; HdCL (Huddersfield district only).
1842. Election of Registrar of Deeds: ByCL, LCL, GL.
1848*. var. BrCL, ByCL, DCL, HdCL, LCL, RCL, SCL, WCL, GL, IHR, MUL, SoG.
1849. YML.
1859. DCL, LCL, WCL, YML, GL, IHR, SoG; HdCL (Huddersfield district only, copy).

Yorkshire West Riding (East)
1868. LCL, Gl.

Yorkshire West Riding (South)
1865. LCL, SCL, WCL, BL, Bod, GL; DCL (Dewsbury only).
1868. DCL, GL, SoG; HdCL (Huddersfield district only).

Beverley
1727. HAO.
1774. GL.
1774. BCL, Hull RO, IHR.
1784. BCL, IHR.
1788. HCL.
1790. BCL, HCL, Hull RO, YML, GL, IHR.
1790, 1791, 1794. Election of Mayor: HAO.
1799*. GL.
1802. var. BCL, HCL, Hull RO, IHR, GL, SoG.
1806. Canvass book: GL.
1806. BCL, HCL, GL, IHR.
1807. BnL.
1807. BCL, HAO, HCL, Hull RO, GL, IHR, SoG.
1807. Election of Mayor: BnL.
1812. BCL, HCL, Hull RO, GL, IHR.

Beverley continued
1818. BCL, HCL, IHR.
1818, 1819, 1820. Election of Mayor: BnL.
1820. var. BCL, HAO, HCL, IHR.
1824*. BCL, HCL.
1824. Election of Mayor: Hull RO.
1826. var. BCL, HAO, HCL, Hull RO, IHR.
1827. Election of Mayor: BnL.
1830. BCL, HAO, HCL, Hull RO, GL, IHR.
1831. BnL.
1831. BCL, IHR, HAO, HCL, Hull RO.
1832. BCL, HCL, IHR.
1835. BnL.
1835. var. BCL, HAO, HCL, Hull RO, IHR.
1837. BnL.
1837. BCL, HAO, HCL, Hull RO, IHR.
1837. Municipal election: HAO, Hull RO.
1840*. BCL, HAO, HCL, Hull RO, GL, IHR.
1841. var. BCL, HAO, HCL, Hull RO, IHR.
1845. Pasture masters election: HCL.
1847. var. BCL, HAO, HCL, Hull RO, Hull UL, Bod, GL, IHR, MCL.
1852. BCL, HAO, HCL, Hull RO, IHR.
1854*. BCL, HAO, HCL, Hull RO, GL, IHR.
1857*. BCL, HAO, HCL, Hull RO, IHR, MCL.
1859. var. BCL, HAO, HCL, Hull RO, GL, IHR.
1860*, 1865. BCL, HAO, HCL, Hull RO, IHR.
1868. var. BCL, HAO, HCL, Hull RO, IHR.
1868. Municipal election. HAO.
1870. Burgess roll with poll added: HCL.

Boroughbridge
1818. IHR.

Bradford
See J.A. Jowitt and R.K.S. Taylor, *Nineteenth Century Bradford Elections* (1979).
1835. DrCL, BrDA, YML, IHR.
1837. BrCL, BrDA, YML, Bod, IHR.
1841 June. var. BrCL, BrDL, YML, Bod, IHR.
1841 Sept. BrCL, BrDA, YML, IHR.
1847. BrCL, IHR.
1852. var. BrCL, YML, IHR.
1859. BrCL, YML, IHR.
1867*. var. BrCL, BLN, IHR.
1868. BrCL, YML, IHR; GL copy with electoral reg.
1869*. BrCL, IHR.
n.d. YML.

Dewsbury
1868. DCL.

Driffield
1869. YML.

Halifax
1832. GL.
1835, 1837, 1841. HxCL, IHR.
1847. var. HxCL, IHR, MCL. See J.A. Jowitt, 'A crossroads in Halifax politics: election of **1847**', *Halifax Antiq. Soc. Trans.* (1973).
1852, 1853*, 1857. HxCL, IHR.

Yorkshire continued
Hedon
1802. HAO, IHR.
1818. GL.
1820. var. BCL, HCL, IHR.
1826. HAO, HCL, IHR.
1837. Hedon district: SoG.

Huddersfield
1834*. HdCL, IHR.
1837*. IHR; HdCL (copy).
1847. HdCL, BL.
1852, 1857. HdCL, HdM, IHR.
1859. Present location unavailable.
1865 (canvass book). HdCL.
1868*. HdCL, IHR.

Kingston-upon-Hull
1723. BL.
1724. Present location unavailable.
1747. HCL.
1747, 1754. Present location unavailable.
1768. NAO, IHR.
1774. BrDA, HCL, GL.
1780, 1784, 1796. HCL, IHR.
1802. HCL, YML, Bod, IHR.
1806. Canvass book: GL.
1806. HCL, BL, Bod, GL, IHR.
1812. HCL, Hull RO, BL, IHR.
1818. var. HCL, Hull RO, BL, Bod, GL, IHR.
1826. HCL, IHR.
1830. HCL, Bod, GL.
1832. var's. HCL, Hull RO, IHR, GL.
1835. var's. HCL, Hull RO, LCL, Bod, GL, IHR.
1835*. HCL, Bod, IHR.
1837. HCL, IHR.
1841. HCL, Hull RO, IHR.
1847. HCL, Hull RO, Bod, IHR.
1852. HCL, Hull RO, Bod, GL, SoG.
1854*. HCL, Hull RO, Bod, GL.
1857. HCL, BL, GL.
1859. HCL, Hull RO, GL.
1859*. HCL, GL.
1865. HCL, Hull RO, GL.
1868. HCL, Hull RO, GL, IHR.

Knaresborough
1841. BrDA, GL.
1857, 1859. GL.

Leeds
1832. LCL, Bod, GL, IHR.
1833 (?). YML.
1834*. LCL, YML, Bod, GL, IHR, SoG.
1835. LCL, GL.
1835. First Municipal election: SoG.
1837. LCL, Bod, GL.
1841. LCL, BL, Bod, GL, IHR, SoG.
1847. LCL, Bod, GL, IHR, MUL.
1852. LCL, YML, Bod, GL, IHR.
1857. LCL, BL, GL, IHR.
1857*. LCL, Bod, GL, IHR.

Leeds continued
1859. LCL, IHR.
1865. LCL, YML, BL, GL.
1868. DCL, LCL, YML, BL, Bod, GL, SoG.

Malton
1807. YML [K.7].

Middlesbrough
1841-49, 1850-52. Election of Commissioners under Middlesbrough Improvement Act: CAM.
1853-58. Election of Councillors etc.: CAM.
1858-69. Election of Councillors, West Ward: CAM.
1858-70. Election of Councillors, North-East and Middle Wards: CAM.
1866-70. Election of Councillors, Boundary Ward: CAM.

Pontefract
1689/90, 1695, 1698, 1699/1700, 1700/01, 1708, 1710, 1713, 1714/5. NUML [Ga 12,259].
1714/5. LDA [BF.9].
1714/5. SRO.
1768. NUML [Ga 12,257-9].
1784. NUML [Ga 12,259].
1847. WCL (on loan).
1852. Bod, IHR.
1857. Bod, GL.
1859, 1860*, 1865, 1868. Bod, IHR.

Richmond
1707. YML [QQ 1.15] (MS?).

Ripon
1832. var. Bod, GL, IHR.
1852, 1865. LDA.
1868. GL.

Scarborough
1835. var. ScCL, IHR, Reading UL.
1837. Bod, IHR.
1852. ScCL, YML, IHR.
1857*, 1859. BLN, IHR.
1860*. var. BLN, IHR.
1865. BLN, IHR.

Sheffield
1832. SCL, YML, Bod, IHR.
1835. SCL, GL, IHR.
1852, 1857. SCL, IHR.

Wakefield
1809. YML.
1835. var. WCL, GL.
1837. var. WCL, GL, NAO.
1841. var. WCL, IHR, GL.
1847. Present location unavailable.
1852. WCL, IHR.
1859 (incl. in 1862 poll). WCL.
1862*, 1865. WCL, IHR.
1868. BLN, IHR.

Yorkshire continued
York
(**1722-41**). See J.F. Quinn, 'York elections in the age of Walpole', *Northern History* **22** (1986).
1722. LDA (incomplete poll book, and check books) [NH.2485, 2494-5].
1741. LDA [NH.2502].
1741. var. LCL, SRO, YML, BL, Bod, GL, IHR.
1742*. YML, Bod [GA 807].
1758*. SRO, YCL, YML, BL, Bod, IHR, SoG.
1774. SRO, YCL, YML, Bod, IHR.
1784. SRO, YCL, YML, BL, Bod, GL, NUL.
1807. var. YCL, YML, BL, Bod, GL, IHR, NUL, SoG.

York continued
1818. SRO, YCL, YML, BL, Bod, GL, IHR.
1820. YCL, YML, BL, Bod, GL, IHR, SoG.
1830. YCL, YML, BL, Bod, GL, IHR, MUL, SoG.
1832. var. YCL, YML, BL, Bod, IHR, GL, SoG.
1835. YCL, YML, BL, Bod, GL, SoG.
1837. HAO, HRO, IHR.
1841. YCL, YML, Bod, IHR.
1852. YCL, YML, Bod, GL, IHR.
1857. YCL, YML, GL, IHR, SoG.
1859. YCL, YML, GL.
1865. YCL, YML, BL, IHR.
1868. YCL, YML, GL, IHR.

WALES and Monmouthshire

In Wales, until 1832, each county returned one member, and Monmouthshire, like other English counties, returned two. Carmarthenshire, Denbighshire and Glamorgan each acquired a second county member in 1832.

For boroughs there was a system whereby most shiretowns shared a member with other 'contributory boroughs' in the same county. These are listed under each constituency:

Further reading:
A.J. James and J.E. Thomas, *Wales at Westminster: A History of the Parliamentary Representation of Wales.* Part 1. *Union to Reform, 1536-1832* (1986); Part 2. *1800-1979* (1981).
R.D. Rees, 'Electioneering ideals current in South Wales **1790-1832**', *Welsh History Review* **2**.3 (1965).
D.A. Wager, 'Welsh politics and parliamentary reform **1780-1832**', *W.H.R.* **7**.4 (1975).
W.R. Williams, *Parliamentary History of the Principality of Wales 1541-1895* (1895).

Abbreviations
ARO = Anglesey Area Record Office (Gwynedd Archives), Llangefni.
Bod = Bodleian Library, Oxford (see page 14).
CaRO = Caernarfon Area Record Office (Gwynedd Archives Service).
CdRO = Ceredigion Record Office (Dyfed Archives), Aberystwyth.
DHRO = Dyfed Record Office, Haverfordwest.
DCRO = Dyfed Record Office, Carmarthen.
GL = Guildhall Library (see page 14).
GRO = Glamorgan Record Office, Cardiff.
GwRO = Gwent County Record Office, Cwmbran.
IHR = Institute of Historical Research (see page 14).
NCL = Newport Central Library.
NLW = National Library of Wales, Aberystwyth. The NLW index does not distinguish between published and unpublished poll books. In this Guide we have assumed the NLW holds MS copies when publication is not known from other sources.
NUML = Manuscripts Department, University of Nottingham.
RCRO = Ruthin Branch, Clwyd Record Office.
SoG = Society of Genealogists (see page 14).
UCNW = University College of North Wales (Department of Manuscripts), Bangor.

ANGLESEY

County
1708. With annotations; and canvass lists: UCNW [B.Hill 5503-25].
1710. UCNW [Pres.497]; also Canvass lists [B.Hill 5503-23].
1754, 1761, 1768. NLW [Esgair & Pantperthog 1113]; Canvass list: UCNW [Pen 1380].
1784, 1837. ARO [WQC/E/157-171].

Anglesey Boroughs (Beaumaris (corporate borough); after 1832, also Amlwch, Holyhead, Llangefni)
1836. Incl. canvass: UCNW [Pen.1384].
1868. Inspector's book: UCNW [Pen.II.922-28].

BRECONSHIRE or BRECKNOCKSHIRE

County
1695, 1702. NLW [Penpont 2394-5].
1734. NLW [Tredegar Park 66/168; 137/399].
1754. NLW [Badminton 11,799; T Pk 33/40, 137/400].
1837. Powys RO [Breconshire Quarter Sessions Q/REp].

Breconshire Boroughs (Brecknock/Brecon, and Llywel)
1727. NLW [T Pk 33/38].

Wales continued

CAERNARVONSHIRE

County
1722. Canvassing return: CaRO.
1740. UCNW [Mostyn 7839].
1768. NLW [Llanfair & Bryndol MS 4]; UCNW [PA.12511-12]; CaRO (Isgwyrfai, Uwchgwyrfai, Arllechwedd Uchef only).
1774. UCNW [PA.12512-23]; Canvassing return: CaRO.
1868. Univ. Coll. of North Wales Library; Inspector's book: UCNW (Central and Western Llyn only: names of voters, how promised, some how polled) [UCNW.712].

Caernarvonshire Boroughs *(Caernarvon, with Conway, Criccieth, Nevon, Pwllheli; after 1832, also Bangor)*
1713. Canvassing return: CaRO (Pwllheli and Nefyn only).
1722. CaRO [Glynllifon 1996]; UCNW [PA.12543].
1784, 1831, 1832. CaRO.
1826. CaRO (Caernarvon only) [Poole Papers].
1831(?). Canvass list: UCNW (probably Caernarvon only) [PA.12578-80].
1833. CaRO (rejected votes only).
1841. Canvass book: UCNW (Caernarvon town only) [PC.B.3721].
1852. Canvassing return: CaRO.
1859. Canvass book: UCNW (Caernarvon town only) [PC.B.3735].

CARDIGANSHIRE

County
(1865, 1868). See I.G. Jones, 'The elections of **1865** and **1868** in Wales with special reference to Cardiganshire and Merthyr Tydfil', *Trans. Hon. Soc. Cymmrodorion* (1964).

Cardiganshire Boroughs *(Cardigan, with Aberystwyth, Lampeter; Tregaron (to 1730); Atpar until 1742, and again from 1832)*
(1547). See P.S. Edwards, 'The mysterious parliamentary election at Cardigan boroughs in 1547', *Welsh History Review* **8** (1976).
(C.18). See P.G.D. Thomas, 'Eighteenth century elections in the Cardigan boroughs constituency', *Ceredigion* **5** (1967).
Early C.19. CdRO [CDM/2/4].
1812. CdRO [CDM/3/5].

CARMARTHENSHIRE

County
1722, 1727. DCRO [Dynevor 160/1,2].
1754. DCRO [Dynevor 160/3, 284/2; Cawdor 1/42]; GL.
1768, 1796. DCRO [Cawdor 1/42, 2/135].
n.d. (C.18). DCRO (Cayo, Derllis, Cathinog, Elvet and the Three Commots only) [Dynevor 160/8].
1796. DCRO [Cawdor 2/135].
1802. NLW (Cayo only) [NLW MS 12169E].
1868. NLW (Llansawel only) [Dolaucothi (uncatalogued)].
1868. NLW, IHR.
1869. NLW (Brunant Estate only) [DTM Jones 3635].

Carmarthenshire Borough(s) *(Carmarthen; after 1832, also Llanelli)*
1796. GL.
1836-46. Elections of Auditors and Assessors, Carmarthen Eastern Ward: DCRO [Museum 4].
1839-46. Elections of Councillors and Aldermen, Carmarthen Eastern Ward: DCRO [Museum 5].
1845-70. DCRO (Carmarthen Eastern Ward) [Museum 6].
1860-70. DCRO (Carmarthen Western Ward) [Museum 7].
1868. NLW [G.E. Owen (uncatalogued)].

DENBIGHSHIRE

County
1716. NLW [Chirk Castle F 838].
1722. NLW [Ch Cas C.12, ?C.13; NLW MS 1619E (transcript by J.P. Earwaker)].
1741. NLW [NLW MS 341.F; Wynnstay L.1298].
1847. NLW [Ch Cas C.97].
1868. NLW [Longueville 790-1]; GL. See J. Morgan, 'Denbighshire's *annus mirabilis*: the borough and county elections of 1868', *Welsh History Review* **7** (1974).

Denbighshire Boroughs *(Denbigh, with Holt, Ruthin; after 1832, also Wrexham)*
1701-1834. Burgess rolls: RCRO (Denbigh Borough only) [BD/A/6-11].
1835-71. RCRO (Denbigh Borough only) [BD/A/245-52].
1837. RCRO (Denbigh, Holt, Ruthin and Wrexham Boroughs) RCRO [BD/A/237-42]; NLW (Holt only) [Ch Cas C.91].
1841. NLW (Holt, mainly) [Ch Cas C.92].
(1868). See J. Morgan, above.

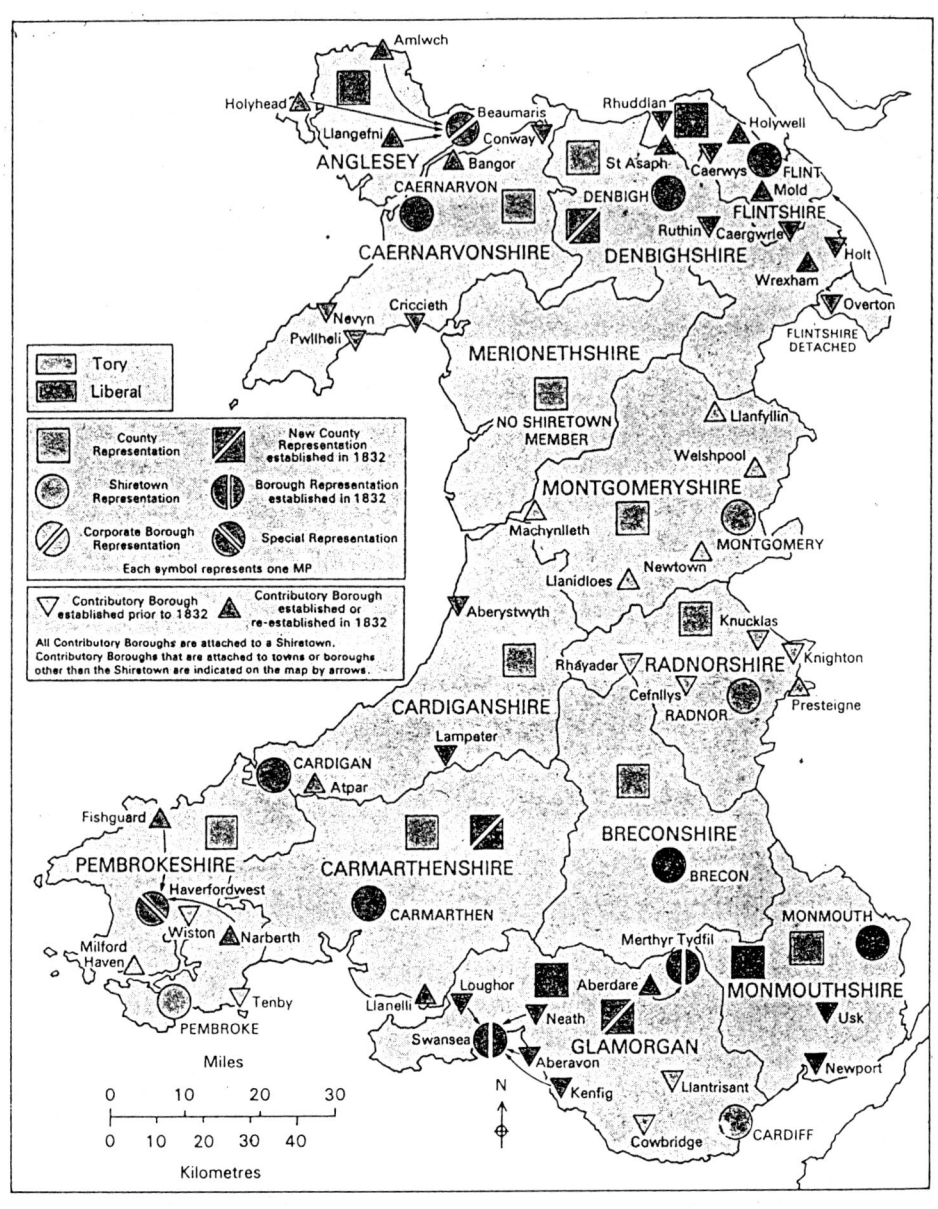

Welsh constituencies before and after 1832 (reproduced from A.J. James and J.E. Thomas, *Wales at Westminster: A History of the Parliamentary Representation of Wales 1800-1979*, Gomer Press, 1981).

Wales continued
FLINTSHIRE
County
1727. UCNW [Mostyn 7883/4].
n.d., first half C.19. NLW [NLW MSS 6319-21.E].

Flintshire Boroughs (Flint, with Caergwrle, Caerwys, Overton, Rhuddlan; after 1832, also Holywell, Mold, St. Asaph)
1727. NLW [Glynne of Hawarden 4952].
1734. Clwyd RO Hawarden; NLW [Wynnstay L.786; G of H 5172-3; Rhual 126-7]; (also Caerwys only) [G of H 5216]; (Overton only) [G of H 5211].
1741. NLW [Wynnstay L.787-8]; (also Flint only) [Wynnstay L.750, 803].
1807. NLW [G of H 4959, 4967, 5001, 5015]; (also Overton and Caergwrle only) [G of H 5011]; UCNW (incl. disallowed voters) [Mostyn 7886-8].

GLAMORGAN
County
1734. NLW [Penrice & Margam 1158; Tredegar Park 34/57]..
1744/5. NLW [T Pk 33/39, 66/169].
1756. GRO.
1820. GRO (excluding Neath Hundred).
1820. Canvass and poll book. NLW
1857. NLW [NLW MS 11906.B].

Glamorgan Boroughs (Cardiff, with Aberavon, Cowbridge, Kenfig, Llantrisant, Neath, Loughor, Swansea; after 1832, Cowbridge and Llantrisant shared with Cardiff, the others joined Swansea, and Merthyr Tydfil had a member, with Aberdare as a contributory borough)
1820. GRO (Cardiff only).
1820. SoG (Cardiff and Kibbor Hundred only).

Merthyr Tydfil
(1835). See G.A. Williams, 'The Merthyr election of 1835', *Welsh History Review* **10** (1981).
(1865, 1868). See I.G. Jones, 'The elections of 1865 and 1868 in Wales with special reference to Cardiganshire and Merthyr Tydfil', *T.H.S. Cym.* (1964).

MERIONETH
County
1768. Canvassing list (fragmentary): CRO [XD2/207-8].

Note. There was no shiretown/borough constituency.

MONMOUTHSHIRE
Formerly adminstratively with England; now Gwent, in Wales.

Constituency histories: Seaton (1986), page 12.
See W.T. Morgan, 'Correspondence relating mainly to Monmouthshire elections 1720-83', *National Library of Wales Journal*, **12**.3 (1962).

County
1703. NLW [Bute 9260].
1705. NLW [Tredegar Park MS 211].
1708. NLW [T Pk MS 211; Bute 9765].
1711. NLW [NLW MS 7660.D (copy)].
1713. NLW [T Pk MS 211]; (Abergavenny only) [T Pk 93/509]; (Caldicot, Skenfrith, Trellick and Ragland only) [T Pk MS 212]; (Trelleck and Ragland only) [T Pk 93/509]; Wentlooge [T Pk 93/509].
1727. NLW [T Pk MSS 211, 213, 253-66].
1771*. NLW [T Pk MSS 229, 231, 232, 247, 53/190-205, 1155]; (Abergavenny only) [T Pk 66/171; T Pk MSS 214-16]; (Caldicot only) [T Pk MSS 217-19]; (Ragland only) [T Pk MSS 220-1]; (Skenfrith only) [T Pk 66/174; T Pk MSS 222-3]; (Trelleck and Ragland only) [T Pk 33/41]; (Usk only) [T Pk 66/173; T Pk MSS 224-5]; (Wentlooge only) [T Pk 66/172; T Pk MSS 226-7].
1771*. NLW [T Pk 18/67]; NCL, IHR, Bod.
1837. NLW [Sir Leonard Twiston-Davies 4941].
1847. GwRO, NCL, Cardiff CL, GL, IHR, NLW.
1868. GwRO, NCL, BL, GL, IHR, NLW, SoG. See T. Colborne, 'Monmouthshire election riots' in *Letters to the Rt. Hon. Henry Austin Bruce, Home Secretary, 1868-69* (1869).

Monmouthshire Boroughs (Monmouth, with Newport, Usk)
1714-5. NCL (the MS is dated 11 Oct. 1714, and the 1906 printed version 12 March 171[4/]5, but they appear to be the same); NLW [NLW MS 7795D: 'transcribed from an original MSS. book belonging to Mr Samuel Dean of Newport'].
1714-5. Reprinted 1906 from NCL MS: Bod, GRO, GL, SoG, Manchester UL.
1771. NLW (Usk only) [Tredegar Park 66/173, MSS 224-5].
1831. NLW [Twiston-Davies 4135-6], (Newport only) [T-D 4139-40].
1831. NCL, IHR.
1832. GwRO (Usk voters only).
1835. GwRO (publ. voters' list, with votes cast unpubl.); NLW [T-D 4727], (Monmouth only) [T-D 4731, 4821], (Newport only) [T-D 4830], (Usk only) [T-D 4831].
1835. NCL, IHR; NLW [T-D 4724].
1837. GwRO (Usk voters only).
1852. NLW (Monmouth voters only) [T-D 5811].
1852. var. NCL, GL, IHR.
1868. NCL, IHR.

Wales: Monmouthshire continued

1869. GwRO (publ. voters' list, with votes cast unpubl.).
n.d. GwRO (Usk voters only).
Monmouth
1824-26. Election of bailiffs: GwRO.
1825 & n.d. Election of Council: GwRO.
1825-26. Election of Mayor: GwRO.
1825-26. Election of Coroner: GwRO.

MONTGOMERYSHIRE

County
(*1656*). See P.D.G. Thomas, 'The Montgomeryshire election of 1656', *Montgomeryshire Collections* **59** (1965/6).
1678/9. NLW (Mathravel only) [Wynnstay L.1199].
1774. NLW [Powis Castle 10620]; (Llanfyllin and Montgomery Hundreds) [Wynnstay L.1248, L.1320]; (also Mathravel only) [Wynnstay L.1247].
1774. GL.
n.d. (C.18). NLW (Llandysul, Aberhafesp, Mochdre, Newtown, Llanllwchaiarn and Ceri only) [Wynnstay L.1315], (Llansantffrraid, Meiford and Llanfechan only) [Wynnstay L.1316].
1832. NLW (Llanidloes only) [Glansevern 14028-37].
(*1728-1868*). See B. Ellis, 'The parliamentary representation of Montgomeryshire **1728-1868**'. *Mont. Coll.* **63.i** (1973).

Montgomeryshire Boroughs (Montgomery; after 1832, also Llanfyllin, Llanidloes, Welshpool (the three restored); Newtown, Machynlleth (both added))
1727. NLW [Montgomery Borough Records 60].
1802. NLW [M.B.R. 66].
1841. 'Estimate of voting': NLW [Cefnbryntalch 478].
1847. Welshpool only: NLW [Wynnstay L.1173].
1847. Welshpool only: NLW, IHR.

PEMBROKESHIRE

County
1765, 1768. NLW [NLW MS 308E (Phillipps MS 13811)].
1807. NLW (Roose only) [NLW MS 6418E].
1812. DHRO [PQ/RP/P/1-7]; NLW (Castlemartin) [6421E], (Narberth) [6420E], (Roose) [6419E].
(*1807, 1812*). See R.G. Thorne, 'The Pembrokeshire elections of 1807 and 1812', *Pembrokeshire Historian* **6** (1979).
1831. DHRO [PQ/RP/P/8-14]; NLW [Eaton, Evans & Williams 4551-7, 4571-8].
1831*. DHRO [PQ/RP/P/15-22]; NLW (Dewsland only) [NLW MS 3010D].

Pembrokeshire Boroughs (Pembroke, with Tenby, Wiston; after 1832, also Milford. Haverfordwest had special representation as it was technically a county (see Introduction, page 5), with, after 1832, Fishguard and Narberth as contributory boroughs)
No poll books known.

RADNORSHIRE

County
(*1604-40*). See J.K. Gruenfelder, 'Radnorshire's parliamentary elections **1604-40**', *Radnorshire Soc. Trans.* **47** (1977).
1690. NUML (Painescastle only) [Pw 2 Hy 400; see also 393-4, 398 for qualifications and disqualifications generally].
1741. NLW [Harpton Court 2503 (copy in a notebook of John Lewis)].
1835. NLW [Cefnbryntalch 481].
1841. NLW (specified districts) [Radnorshire Quarter Sessions S.1023-30].

Radnorshire Boroughs ((New) Radnor, with Cefnllys, Knighton, Knucklas, Rhayadr; after 1832, also Presteign)
(*1690*). See J.A. Downie, 'Robert Harley, Sir Rowland Gwynne and the New Radnor election of 1690', *Radnors. S.T.* **46** (1976).
1727. 'New Radnor...' Bod [GA Radnor b.1]; NLW [NLW Facsimile 353].
1802. NLW (Rhayader only) [Glansevern 14050].

SCOTLAND

Abbreviations
ECL = Edinburgh Central Library (Scottish Room).
IHR = Institute of Historical Research (see page 14).
NLS = National Library of Scotland.
SoG = Society of Genealogists.
SRO = Scottish Record Office.

In Scotland from 1707 to 1832 the County voting franchise was much more restricted than in England and Wales (see Introduction). In 1788 there were only 2,662 voters in all. Most elections were unopposed. Thus there are virtually no pre-1832 poll books as such. However, for the years **1788**, **1790**, **1811** and **1812** there are printed books listing all the freeholders county by county, showing the way they voted in the few contested elections. These are:

Sir Charles Elphinston Adam (ed.), *A View of the Political State of Scotland in the last century: A confidential report on the ... 2,662 County Voters about **1788***, Edinburgh (1887) (from a MS report to aid the Rt. Hon. William Adam of Blair Adam and Henry Erskine in managing the interests in Scotland of the Whig opposition to Pitt and Henry Dundas).

A. Mackenzie, *A View of the Political State of Scotland at the late general election: Rolls of Freeholders ... as made up at the meetings for choosing their Representatives ... July **1790***.

James Bridges, *View of the Political State of Scotland at Michaelmas **1811** comprehending the rolls of the Freeholders (made up at the Michaelmas Head Counts)*, Edinburgh, John Moir (1812). In the same volume, lists made up in **1812** with names expunged or added. They were apparently altered each year at the meeting, as people had died or freeholds were bought or sold.

There are copies at ECL and NLS; also, for 1788 at SRO and SoG; and for 1790 at IHR.

In the following list elections are for the County unless shown otherwise.

ABERDEENSHIRE

1807. Publ. in *Aberdeen Journal Notes and Queries*. 1, p.147.

ANGUS

Dundee Burgh
(**1806**). See Jupp 1973.
1865/6. Dundee Archive and Record Centre.

ARGYLL

1837. Tobermory only. SRO (West Register House) [SC54/22/128].

Ayr, Banff, Berwick, Bute, Caithness: no poll books known.

CLACKMANNAN

1832-1851. SRO [SC64/63/37-41].

CROMARTY

(**1769**?) See *State of the election for the County of Cromarty, in North Britain* (1769?).
1832-1895. *States of the polls...* SRO [SC24/21/3].

DUMFRIES

(**1708, 1710**). See *State of the election of the Shire of Dumfries* (1708); similar for 1710.
1868. var. SoG.
1869*. SoG.

Dumfries
(**1806**). See Jupp 1973.
1832, 1833, 1836, 1840-51, 1854-56, 1858-60, 1862-65, 1867, 1869. Municipal elections (various wards): Dumfries Archive Centre [GOLD/H.3/51-78].

DUNBARTON

(**1821**). See Jupp 1973.

East Lothian (Haddingtonshire), **Fife:** no poll books known.

INVERNESS

Fort William District
1832, 1835, 1835[A]. SRO [SC/29/71/8-15].

Inverness Burghs
(**1806**). See Jupp 1973.

Inverness District
1832, 1835. SRO [SC/29/71/10,11].

Kingussie District
1835. SRO [SC/29/71/14].

Skye District
1832, 1835. SRO [SC/29/71/8,9].

Kincardine, Kinross: no poll books known.

KIRKCUDBRIGHT

Castle Douglas polling place
1841, 1845. SRO [SC/16/68/8,9].

Kirkcudbright polling place
1841, 1845. SRO [SC/16/68/6,7].

New Galloway polling place
1841, 1845. SRO [SC/16/68/10,11].

Scotland continued

LANARK
1818. IHR.
1832, 1835. Duke of Hamilton (c/o N.R.A. Scotland).

Lanark Burghs
(1806). See Jupp 1973.

Glasgow
1832. Mitchell Library, Glasgow; NLS, IHR, Manchester CL.

LINLITHGOW (West Lothian)
(1726). See *The case of the election of the Shire of Linlithgow* (1726).

MIDLOTHIAN
Edinburgh
(1806). See Jupp 1973.
1847. ECL, IHR.
1852. ECL, GL, IHR.

Moray, Nairn, Orkney: no individual poll books known.

PEEBLES
Innerleithen, Linton and *Peebles*
1868. SRO [SC/42/44/1-4].

PERTH
1790. NLS, IHR.

RENFREW
1832. IHR.

ROSS and CROMARTY
Dingwall Burghs
(1806). See Jupp 1973.

ROXBURGH
1780. NLS, IHR. See *Minutes of meeting of freeholders ... 1780 for the purpose of electing their representative in Parliament* (1780?).
1868. Annotated electoral reg. NLS [Douglas of Springwood Park Kelso papers 8119].

SELKIRK
Galashiels and Selkirk
1832, 1835, 1837, 1846, 1861, 1865. SRO [SC/63/62/1-15].

Shetland: no poll books known.

STIRLING
Airdrie District
1841, 1851*, 1852, 1865. SRO [SC.67/61/113-19].

Culross
1852, 1868. SRO [SC.67/61/97-98].

Drymen District
1832, 1835, 1837, 1841, 1865. SRO [SC.67/61/69-78].

Dunfermline Burgh
1852, 1868*, 1868. SRO [SC.67/61/85-89].

Falkirk
1851*, 1852, 1865. SRO [SC.67/61/99-101].

Falkirk District
1832, 1835, 1837, 1841, 1865. SRO [SC.67/61/50-58].

Hamilton
1841, 1851*, 1852, 1865. SRO [SC.67/61/109-12].

Inverkeithing
1852, 1868*, 1868. SRO [SC.67/61/91-93].

Lanark
1841, 1851*, 1852, 1865. SRO [SC.67/61/102-05].

Lennoxtown District
1832, 1835, 1837, 1841, 1865. SRO [SC.67/61/59-68].

Linlithgow
1851*, 1852, 1865. SRO [SC.67/61/106-08].

Queensferry
1852, 1868*, 1868. SRO [SC.67/61,94-96].

Stirling Burgh
1852, 1868*, 1868 Nov. SRO [SC.67/61/79-84].

Stirling District
1832, 1835, 1837, 1841, 1865. SRO [SC.67/61/40-49].

Sutherland: no individual poll books known.

West Lothian: see Linlithgow.

WIGTOWN
1835-1841. SRO [SC19/64/3-7] (Mss?).

Wigtownshire Upper District
1868. SRO [Agnew of Lochnaw Muniments GD 154/611].